See What's Yucky Inside

W9-AYJ-829

Acknowledgments

Ihave a confession. After writing this book, I don't get as "grossed out" as much. For instance, I used to be revolted when I found globs of phlegm in the sink. Now, I don't recoil in disgust; I'm merely annoyed that I have to clean it! And sure, vomit isn't pretty, but when I see a patch on the sidewalk or in the corner of a parking lot, I'm curious as to whether it's the chunky, barely digested kind or the smooth chyme ready to be absorbed in the small intestine by eager microvilli.

Maybe I've always had a penchant for the unusual. My father, after all, is a forensic pathologist and performed autopsies for a living. My sisters and I grew up with stories of dissection over dinner and shelves full of gory, real-life murder mystery books. There aren't that many books on the library shelves about those things we find repugnant. The list is slowly growing, though. Just accepting the fact that there is a gross and disgusting aspect of our bodies is half the battle. Yep, the "grossities" exist, so you might as well admit it—and a laugh or two never hurts, either. Writing this book has been an eye-opening experience and a great deal of fun. I hope you have as much fun reading it as I did researching and writing it!

DEDICATION

For Veronica, Montgomery and Miriam, a.k.a. VeeVee, Monty and Mimi!

There are so many people I would like to thank for making this book possible. Thanks to my publisher, Blue Bike Books; project director, Nicholle Carrière; and my editor, Kathy van Denderen, for all their help. I would also like to thank a whole bunch of other people including (but not limited to!) the two doctors, David King and Caroline King; supportive friends Nick Reiter, April Hayward, Mark Cuddy and, of course, Mark Innes; as well as HTZ-FM's awesome DJ, Kristy Knight. A huge thanks goes out to my family, and especially to my patient husband, Greg Emery. I'm so glad all of you have a great sense of humor!

Introduction

When I was in kindergarten, our class learned all about the parts of the body. Head and shoulders, knees and toes, it was all there, except some things were missed or at least glossed over. When we talked about hair, we didn't mention dandruff. We each had a nose, but what about the boogers that clumped up inside it? We could feel our teeth with our tongues, but weren't cavities hiding in there, too? We learned about skin, but why was the giant mole on the teacher's nose ignored? Yes, there's more to you and me than meets the eye. The human body is fascinating, and many people describe it as a remarkable machine. But when was the last time you saw a machine fart or throw up? No doubt about it, we all have a gross side!

Humans are among the few animals that find certain things disgusting. There's probably a good reason for that, and it likely has to do with evolution. For instance, most cultures in the world think vomit is gross. Why is vomit disgusting? Well, it looks like puke. It is puke. And someone puked it up for a reason. We think "EWWW!" and get away from that puke as fast as we can in case we get the same infection. It's the same with poop. Poop, especially human poop, is full of bacteria. Touching or eating it can make us very sick indeed.

So when exactly is something truly gross? A mole on the nose might look repugnant to one person but perfectly normal to someone else. Sure, nobody wants to pluck out eye crud or see boogers hanging off someone's nose, but is that truly disgusting? Or is it just plain ugly? People spend a huge amount of time trying not to be gross. We don't pick our noses in front of a new date. We hide those pimples and dark undereye circles with concealer. We try to be discreet about farting and belching in public (well, most of us, anyway). And if the urge to puke sneaks up on us, given the choice, most of us will run to a bathroom stall instead of expelling our lunch all over the buffet table. As hard as we try, we can't escape gross. And when you can't beat 'em, join 'em! Or at least try to learn as much as you can....

The Building Blocks of GROSS

The Gross Factor

It's a fact of life. The human body can be gross and disgusting. So can birds, animals, insects, or your cat or dog. When my cat leaves a mushy hair ball on the kitchen floor and I step on it, I find that very gross. Everything, from the smallest animal to your great-grandfather, grows, pukes, pees, reproduces—you name it, we do it. Simply carrying out these functions means we are alive.

> The human body can be gross and disgusting.

If you become that lucky one out of 2 billion people who live to be 116 years old or more, you'll have endured a lot of gross and embarrassing situations. For instance, in that lifetime, you'll have farted over half a million times! You will have had your fair share of stinky feet, bad body odor,

putrid pimples and zillions of other revolting bodily
functions. To understand the how and why about these
gross and disgusting things our bodies do, we need to
start with the smallest parts. Most are so tiny, they're
microscopic. These are the cells, bacteria and viruses...the
mighty microbes of "gross"!

The BLOB, a.k.a the CELL

What are little boys made of?
Frogs and snails and puppy dogs' tails.

What are little girls made of?
Sugar and spice and everything nice.

It's an old rhyme, but children, or adults for that matter, aren't made of amphibians, canine parts or baked goods. We are all made of cells. About 10 **trillion** of them. There are about 200 different types of cells in the human body. Like a factory with different departments, each type has a special job to do. Cells are so tiny, you need a microscope to see them. Ten cells could probably fill the diameter of one strand of hair from your head. It's probably a good thing cells are so small. When you view a cell for the first time, it is one strange-looking blob.

Peeking Inside the Blob, er, Cell

An Englishman named Robert Hooke first used the term "cells" in 1665 when describing the structure of cork. In 1673, a Dutch scientist named Anton von Leeuwenhoek peered into his own homemade microscope. He was able to see tiny creatures that had since been invisible to the human eye. As science progressed, researchers learned more about bacteria and cells.

Each cell has a membrane that surrounds it and holds everything in. Molecules can pass in and out of this membrane. Like our bodies, cells contain organs. They were so teeny-weeny that these organs became known as organelles, which float around in a watery fluid called cytoplasm. There are also enzymes that, like crazy scientists, love to carry out chemical reactions. Enzymes take molecules and put them together, or break them apart, so cells can grow, reproduce, create energy and even make other enzymes. Cells also excrete enzymes; that is, they kick out the ones they don't need anymore.

In the middle of a plant or animal cell is a control center called the nucleus. Inside that are things that look similar to bits of thread called chromosomes. They are found in all our human cells except red blood cells. Chromosomes contain DNA (deoxyribonucleic acid), which is something you might have heard about in newspapers or on TV. The DNA molecule looks like a twisted ladder, and it contains all the information a cell needs to function. DNA contains genes— not "jeans" as in your favorite pair of pants, but genes as in genetic material.

DiD YOU KNOW?

Three billion cells in your body die every minute, but just as many are replaced in the same time.

When a cell divides into two, the DNA makes a copy of itself so the second new cell can carry out the same functions as the original one did. You've got the same DNA in all the cells of your body. Thankfully, some parts of the DNA can be switched off. If it didn't, your cells would be very mixed up indeed. You might end up with eye cells that would try to hear, or brain cells that wanted to make hair. It's a very scary thought.

Welcome to the JUNGLE

Yes, there are more bacteria on Earth than people, horses, cows, mosquitoes, ladybugs, you name it. We can't see bacteria, but they're everywhere. Yep, you can't do anything, eat anything—you can't really exist—without running into bacteria. They've been around a long, long time, too. Not only millions but **billions** of years. And billions live on you and in you.

It's a jungle out there. A jungle of microscopic organisms. But...it's also a flower garden. Say what?

In the same way that Paris Hilton totes her pet dog all over, we carry our bacteria with us everywhere we go. Much of the bacteria in us, like the bacteria in our gut, are good guys. They are part of the normal flora of the human body. That's "flora" as in flower. It's as if you have a garden of bacteria growing right under your nose (and other places).

Bacteria come in different shapes—round, rod-shaped, bent or even spiral. And like flowers, they often come in different colors,

Question:
What is the dominant life form on our planet?

Answer:
Bacteria!

14

such as blue or green (though I haven't seen a green flower petal lately).

What are bacteria? Each one, called a bacterium, is a complete living cell. It lives. It eats. It excretes. It loves to multiply. Just like our cells, a bacterium has a cell membrane that surrounds it. The difference between cells and bacteria is that a bacterium doesn't have cytoplasm or a nucleus. Some bacteria are anaerobic, meaning that they prefer to live in places with very little oxygen, such as in the intestine or the tiny, hidden spaces within the mouth. Others simply prefer to sit on our skin, multiplying away until we wash them off. We can never completely wash them away, of course. That's why bacteria are always with you. Get used to it.

Pirate Viruses

Bacteria, like viruses, are microscopic. If it came to a size contest, though, viruses would lose. They are smaller than bacteria, and they can't move around by themselves. Unlike bacteria and other cells, viruses don't grow or eat, so technically they aren't even alive.

Viruses may seem like tiny losers, but they can pack a pretty mean punch. They are tiny invaders that take over a cell, usually

your cells. Like pirates, they jump onto the ship (the cell) and kick off all the sailors (the DNA). Once they've taken over a cell, viruses use it for what they want, namely to reproduce themselves. The poor cell, now full of viruses, breaks open, and out rush the new viruses. They, in turn, take over more cells and so on, and so on.

We've all had run-ins with viruses. If you've ever had a cold or the flu, you've caught a virus. The common cold is caused by viruses (such as adenovirus or coronavirus). They enter the body through the nose, eyes and tear ducts. Chicken pox, cold sores, measles and mumps are caused by viruses, too. There also are worse and more deadly viruses out there, such as HIV (human immunodeficiency virus), the virus that can cause AIDS (acquired immune deficiency syndrome).

The War at Home

Usually, our body can cope with those things we call germs—the bad bacteria and viruses. Our skin acts as a barrier and keeps most of them out. We have mucus to trap bacteria, and bodily fluids to wash them away. We also have tiny bacteriophages (also called phages), which are microbes that infect and kill germs. When our body detects too many of these bad guys in one place, it sends in the hired help.

THE BUILDING BLOCKS OF GROSS

Sometimes, doctors might prescribe an antibiotic to fight an infection. Antibiotics attack germs, and the first antibiotic, penicillin, was discovered in 1928 by Sir Alexander Fleming of Scotland. Since then, antibiotics have saved millions of lives. For instance, during World War I, nearly 20 percent of soldiers with pneumonia died. By the time antibiotics were used during World War II, the number had dropped to less than one percent.

If you've ever had a Cold or the Flu, you've caught a Virus.

The use of vaccines is the modern way to fight disease. Injecting a tiny amount of a virus or bacteria into the body allows us to develop immunity to that disease.

As you can see, the human body is in constant yellow alert against vile viruses and bacteria that might harm us.

So what does all this have to do with the gross and disgusting things that happen in your body? Well, when it comes to viruses and germs, your body goes into defense mode to fight them off. The effects can be rather revolting, but necessary. The same thing happens when bad bacteria invade your system. Usually, we can fight them on our own, but sometimes we need help from modern medicine.

There is, however, another more common and ordinary function that occurs as a result of bacteria. It's not as dangerous as infection or disease, but it's a biggie when it comes to gross. What is it? In a word, excretion.

What Goes In, Must Come Out

Microscopic bacteria love to eat the cells on our body, especially the dead ones. Bacteria, like other life forms, produce waste products. Our bodies make solid, liquid and gas waste (in other words, poop, pee and farts), but bacteria's waste is much simpler—it's made up of chemical compounds. Most of these chemicals have a distinct odor. Usually, the odors are not particularly lovely.

For instance, two types of bacteria that are found on human skin, cornybacteria and brevibacteria, love to munch on dead skin cells. After a big meal, these bacteria sit around and digest. What they can't use, they excrete,

COUGH COUGH

and in their case, it's methane thiol. Methane thiol is a colorless gas, but it stinks. When you happen to smell dog crap (after all, who hasn't accidentally stepped in doggie doo-doo?), you smell the methane thiol. Interestingly, it is also the same chemical that gives stinky Limburger cheese its overpowering odor.

Now, what something smells like is often different for different people. If I shove a smelly old sock in your face, you might describe it as having a rotten fish odor. I, however, might say it reminds me of cheesy sandwiches left in a locker for three days. In general, scientists have identified the odor of certain chemical compounds:

Isovaleric acid – a sweaty feet smell, but can also have the odor of rancid cheese

Hydrogen sulfide – stinks like rotten eggs

Dimethyl disulfide – smells like rotten cabbage

Methane thiol – pungent cheesy smell

Methyl mercaptan – smells like dirty socks or rotten cabbage; some say it smells cheesy; it also gives that awful smell to skunk secretions

Butyric acid – rancid butter smell

Amine compounds – usually a fishy odor

As you can see, knowing that bacteria excrete is one key factor to understanding gross, at least, the smelly factor. It's all in the chemistry. Now that you know the basics of cells and germs, let's explore all the gross and disgusting— yet fascinating—things about our body!

Ewww!

Mysophobia is the fear of germs. Howard Hughes, the famous 20th-century aviator and entrepreneur, had it and wore gloves all the time.

YUCK from the NECK UP

Racking your BRAIN

If you went by looks, it might be more attractive to have a sleek, black laptop instead of a brain inside your skull. Face it, we should be grateful we can't see our brain through our heads. Imagine a pink, spongy but solid mass of compact tubes that looks as though it just came out of your guts. Now picture it floating on top of a stem—your brain stem—that connects to your spinal cord. Make sure the brain and spinal cord are all web-connected with neurons—those wire-looking cells that zap off electrical signals. Throw in a mass of blood vessels, to supply the brain cells with blood and all its goodies, and you've got yourself "brains." Yep, it's all in your head...literally. Without your brains acting as the command center for the rest of your body...well, you'd be dead.

Fortunately, we usually don't see our gross-looking brains; they're hidden and protected by eight bones that make up the cranium. We're hard-headed, so to speak, except when we're babies. A newborn's skull has gaps between the cranium bones, called the fontanelles. We sometimes call these gaps the "soft spots" on a baby's head. When a baby is born, the bones squeeze together so that the baby has an easier time getting through the birth canal. Afterwards, the baby's brain grows incredibly fast, and it takes a year and a half before the cranium bones actually fuse together.

Pickled Brains

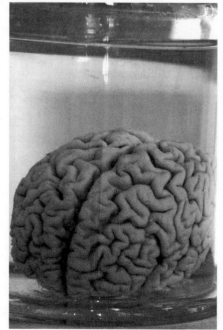

You've probably seen one in a horror movie—a wrinkly, grayish, pickled brain floating in a jar on a mad scientist's laboratory shelf. A living brain doesn't look much different, except it's more pink than gray. It is more than 80 percent water, too. Everyone's brain has an outer covering called the dura mater, which is Latin for "hard mother,"

but it's not as hard as the bone that protects the brain. And as hard as the skull is, it still needs a helmet when we do things such as biking or bungee jumping.

Parts of an Egghead

The biggest part of your brain is the cerebrum. This is where all your thoughts, feelings and movements are computed. The cerebrum is divided into two halves: the left hemisphere and the right hemisphere. Here's where the situation gets confusing. The right half of your brain mainly controls the

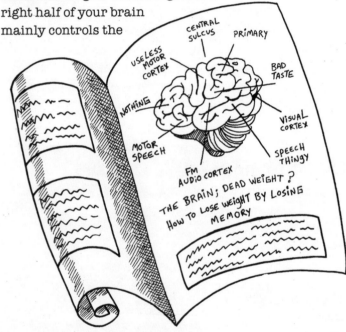

left side of your body. The left half of your brain mainly controls the right side of your body. If you raise your right hand, the message to do so travels through the left part of your brain. Talk about mixed up!

The outer part of the cerebrum is the "cerebral cortex." Its name is Latin for "bark," as in the bark of a tree. Most people call it "gray matter." The cerebral cortex is divided into four lobes: frontal, temporal, parietal and occipital. They are covered in bumps and cracks, which give the cerebral cortex an ugly, wrinkly appearance. These bumps (the gyri) and the grooves or cracks (the sulci) aren't just for hideous looks, they allow more brain tissue to be packed into a smaller area. If you laid out the cerebral cortex, its surface area would be as large as one sheet of newspaper. Much better to scrunch it up and stuff it in a skull.

At the back of the brain, under the cerebrum, sits the cerebellum, or "little brain." It's small but important, because it controls balance and coordination. In front of the cerebellum is the brain stem, which connects the brain to the spinal cord. Breathing, digestion, blood circulation—they're all the work of the brain stem. Near the top of the brain stem is the hypothalamus, which acts as a thermostat and keeps your body at the right temperature, 98.6°F. Your brain also has an amygdala that helps control emotions. The word "amygdala" comes from the Greek for "almond," because it looks similar to one.

Brain Juice

Right now, your brain is afloat. It's not exactly bobbing around, but it is suspended in a clear, colorless liquid called cerebrospinal fluid (or CSF). This wet stuff works like a cushion within the ventricles, or spaces, of your brain and in the soft brain tissue between your skull and spinal cord. You have about five ounces of CSF in your brain right now, and approximately two cups are produced by your brain every day.

CSF keeps everything at the right pressure and absorbs any shocks that come along. Your brain weighs a lot less when it floats around in CSF. Otherwise, the average brain tips the scales at about three pounds. That's a little less than a dolphin's brain but 100 times heavier than a rabbit's brain. It would take at least four human brains to weigh as much as one elephant brain. Men have slightly bigger brains than women but that doesn't mean they are smarter. Oh, and one other thing—after the age of 30, the brain shrinks by about one-quarter of a percent each year.

Spindly Neurons

When it comes to doing quick calculations, the computer wins over the brain, hands down. You have to give credit to the brain, though. It usually doesn't crash and hasn't required an upgrade for millennia! Your cerebellum contains more than half of all the brain's neurons, which are billions of nerve cells that carry electrical signals. And they work quickly, sending signals that can zoom around faster than the fastest car on a racetrack. It's a pretty tangled path they take too...a real maze. Your neurons take incoming and outgoing messages. They can do this because they have branch-like signal receivers called dendrites (from the Greek word for "tree"), and conductors called axons.

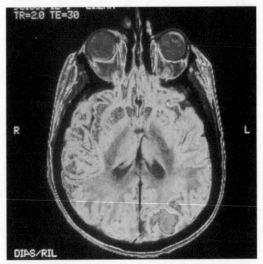

Axons, or nerve fibers, are bound together like wires in a telephone cable. Their endings, the axon terminals, send messages across a gap, called a synapse, to the next cell. Each neuron has about 1000 to 10,000 synapses, meaning it communicates with that many cells. If you think that's a big number, imagine this: There are about 60 trillion synapses in the cerebral cortex, and one quadrillion (that's a 1 followed by 15 zeros) in the brain!

Old Brains

Why do grandparents keep asking you the same, boring questions over and over again? Blame it on their brains. If you are under 18 years old, your brain is still growing and making new connections. As you get older, some of those neuron connections quit working. Keeping your brain active helps to prevent this. So get out those memory games and crossword puzzles, or learn a new language. You need every brain cell you've got!

Dazed and Confused

If your brain doesn't receive enough blood, you could feel dizzy, and PLONK! You've just fainted (also called syncope). It's your body's way of telling you to lie down and to send the brain some blood—pronto!

When you have a headache (cephalagia), it's not the brain that hurts, it's the membranes, blood vessels and muscles in your scalp and around your brain that feel the pain. Migraines are severe headaches that can last for hours or days. Just be glad you don't live in the Middle Ages. The cure for headaches back then was trepanning, which involved cutting out a piece of the skull to relieve the pressure!

Brain Farts

You hear a song on the radio. Now name the band that plays it. You know it but can't remember it just now, right? Oops, you've just had a brain fart. It's a crude way of saying you are "drawing a blank." When this happens, there is actually a lapse in your brain thought process. If you hear someone say, "Oh, the answer is on the tip of my tongue," he or she is having a brain fart. There are other examples, but I can't remember them right now.

People Who Taste Words

This is a weird one—synesthesia—a condition that occurs when your senses get crossed. Some people see colors when they hear a certain sound, or even "taste" words. It's a mouthful, but "tasting words" is called lexicalgustatory synesthesia. I'm sure you are wondering how on earth someone can taste a word. Well, we all make word associations. If I say "chocolate," you can imagine what it tastes like. Synesthetes (people with synesthesia) put a different slant on those associations. The taste sensation is triggered by the meaning of a word. For these people, when they hear food names, such as "mint," they actually taste mint.

For other words, it seems that the sounds within the word set off the sense. For instance, words containing an "aye" sound would taste like bacon. Researchers think that synesthesia occurs in about one in 2000 people, and the majority of them are women. Most people with synesthesia don't mind having it, though one researcher spoke of a study participant who complained that when he was driving and trying to read street signs, he'd have the sensation of tasting earwax. I wonder how he knew what earwax tasted like?

Can't Place that Face?

Hmm. That girl over there looks familiar. I know I've met her before, I just can't remember her name. Oh, maybe it will come to me. Or maybe I should admit to her that I've forgotten her name.

NEAT!

The brain is one demanding organ and uses more energy for its size than any other organ in the body. It uses as much energy as a 20-watt lightbulb and about 15 to 20 percent of the body's oxygen.

Has this ever happened to you? It's not uncommon, and it usually happens with people we don't know very well.

But what if it's someone you do know well? What if you could never tell who a person was simply by looking at his or her face? Prosopagnosia is the inability to identify familiar faces. The condition is also called face-blindness and is often the result of an injury to the brain. A person with this condition has no vision problems and can **see** a face. The problem is that he or she doesn't recognize who the face belongs to.

Brain Food

When you eat shrimp, are you eating their brains? Sort of, but in this case, "brains" are better described as a clump of nerve cells. Lobster, crabs and other shellfish have the same sort of thing. Jellyfish, however, don't have brains. And the next time you are in a delicatessen, ask for a few slices of headcheese. You'll be given a cold-cut delicacy made from jellied pig brains!

NOSY About the NOSE

Thank heavens for noses. Sure, yours may look like a honker, but it's a very useful body part. Every day you breathe over 23,000 times through one or both nostrils—those two holes at the end of your nose divided by a piece of thick skin called the septum. The word "nostril" comes from the Old English "nosthryl," which means "nose hole."

Weird, but true, is that the diameter of each nostril just happens to be about the same size as your fingertip, which brings us to boogers—those clumps of gunk that fingers often pull out of our noses.

Booger City

A "booger," also known as snot, nose gob and so on, is a chunky bit of dried mucus (though each one looks different, and parts of it can be moist, flexible, stringy or very oddly shaped).

Where does a booger come from? Your body's mucus factory. Mucus is a very important slippery and slimy substance. It traps bacteria and generally keeps your internal body parts from drying out. Mucus is mostly water, so it looks similar to the stuff you pump out of a liquid soap dispenser, but thicker mucus can remind you of a glob of glue or jelly that's been left outside too long.

Mucus is also chock-full of special antiseptic enzymes and other goodies that protect the organs it slides over. As it moves along, mucus picks up bacteria, germs, bits and pieces of dirt and dust, among other things. The goal of mucus is to shove all these impurities out of the body to keep it healthy. This explains why you seem to have more mucus when you're sick (such as with a cold)—your body is trying to get rid of the extra germs, so it produces more mucus and therefore expels more.

Mucus is found in your lungs, stomach, intestines, reproductive system and in a whole bunch of other body parts. It's made in special tissue, the mucosal membrane. Apart from your nasal cavity, mucus in your throat and lungs (the respiratory system) is phlegm. If you cough up phlegm (some people call it "hawking a loogie" or "horking a gob"), it's called sputum.

Doing the Wave

Your nasal mucus (mucus in your nose) is shoved along to the back of your throat by tiny, whip-like hairs called cilia. They're found on the walls of the nasal cavity and are not to be confused with the larger nose hairs from the front part of your nostrils (if you've ever inspected a booger, you've probably seen one or two of those ugly nose hairs welded inside).

Cilia "do the wave" about 1500 times a minute as they push the mucus along. Mucus moves much more slowly in the nostrils, trapping dirt and debris. Because it's cooler in the nose, the mucus thickens and dries into a blob—the booger.

It then sits there, waiting to be picked out by a finger, which happens to be just the right size.

Most of the mucus from your nose eventually ends up in your esophagus (or windpipe) and gets swallowed. In your stomach, the mucus is digested, and so are the bacteria. Sometimes, though, the mucus flies out of the body during sternutation. You've done it, your dog's done it, everyone's done it—sternutation, that is, or as it's commonly called, sneezing.

Achoo to You, Too!

A lot of junk can get shoved up those nostrils (and I don't mean marbles, peas or bits of tissue paper). It's usually dust, allergens or temperature changes that bother the inside of your nose to the point where the cilia react.

One in four people have photic sneezing (that is, sneezing when you go out in the sun), and the problem seems to run in families. Even eyebrow plucking can tickle the sensitive nerves in the lining of your nose. When these nerves are stimulated, a message is sent through the spinal cord to your brain to do something, quick. Your muscles then contract and relax until there's one big expulsion and you've sneezed. Whatever is in your nose is expelled at a speed of over 100 miles per hour, and a sneeze droplet can land 30 feet away from you!

The muscles involved in sneezing include those in your chest, diaphragm, face and eyes (which is why your eyes close when you sneeze). If your mouth is open, you can blow out chunks of whatever was loose in there. Usually that's saliva or throat mucus, but it could be half-chewed food or even dentures.

What's crazier is that when you sneeze, everything in your body seems to stop momentarily. Some even think your heart skips a beat. No wonder people say "bless you" after a sneeze. They probably want to make sure your heart starts up again. Actually, the phrase dates back all the way to the sixth century when illnesses such as the bubonic plague often started with a sneeze. Traditionally, it was thought that your soul escaped your body during a sneeze, and saying "God bless you" would keep the devil from taking your soul before it could get back safely. "Gesundheit," another customary response to hearing a sneeze, is a German word and means "good health," which sounds a lot more logical.

So the next time you sneeze, whether it's once or twice, or three times (or more), just be glad you are not Donna Griffiths of Worcestershire, UK. She holds the world record for sneezing—978 days in a row, starting in 1983. She sneezed over a million times during the first year alone!

I'm All Thuffed Up

The air that enters through your nose and into your lungs has to be at the right temperature and the right humidity. If the air is too dry, too hot or too cold, your lung tissues won't be happy campers. Your nasal and sinus cavities

YUCK!

During the Middle Ages, phlegm was one of the four humors, or special fluids, in the body. If a humor was out of balance, you got sick. Too much phlegm made a person sluggish, even unemotional. They were "phlegmatic." Besides phlegm, the other humors were blood, black bile and yellow bile.

have glands that produce fluid to coat the mucous membranes. If it's very dry outside, the mucus gets too thick. The cilia don't sweep as well, and you get globs of mucus in your nose that drip out (so wipe your nose!). If the sinuses get clogged, pressure builds up. The mucus doesn't move, bacteria grows and the next thing you know, you have a sinus infection, or sinusitis.

That Smells Like . . .

Ever wondered why we have two nostrils instead of one? Two come in handy when you've got a cold and one is all stuffed up. Besides increasing air intake for breathing, two nostrils make our sense of smell better, too.

At the top of your nasal cavity, in a space the size of a postage stamp, are some 10 million smell receptor cells. These special sensor cells detect the different chemicals in smells and send the information to your brain. Most people can distinguish up to 10,000 different odors, and women are usually better at it than men.

As each smell enters our nasal cavity, it gets involved in a chemical reaction with each receptor cell; some are fast-acting, others take a longer time. Usually, one nostril has faster airflow than the other. In other words, we've all got a slowpoke nostril and a speedy one. Fast-acting smells are often picked up first by the nostril with the faster airflow. The slower ones stay in the other nostril. This means you can savor more smells. The key word here is "savor," because by smelling something, some of the odor's molecules have interacted with taste receptor cells at the back of your throat. In a sense (no pun intended), you've actually tasted the smell, too, which is good if it's something delicious, such as freshly baked bread—and not so good if it's, well, a fart.

The Bogey Ball

For two years, an English artist collected his boogers in the name of art. Squishing them together, he eventually created a "Bogey Ball" the size of a brussels sprout and placed it in an eggcup. He even exhibited the ball at various art exhibitions. Since boogers are made of dust and skin, the artwork was, in his words, "a physical record of all the different places he had been and people he had met."

Picky, Picky

You've probably sat beside someone who is always picking his or her nose. (Caution: Do not run your hand under that person's desk; it could be the secret hiding place where the boogers are stashed.) Compulsive nose-picking is called rhinotillexomania. The act of sticking a finger up the nose and pulling out a booger is called rhinotillexis. If you eat it, you've just committed mucophagy.

Here's a shocker: Dr. Friedrich Bischinger, an Austrian lung specialist, believes eating boogers may be beneficial for the human body. He has publicly stated that society should encourage nose picking:

"With the finger, you can get to places you just can't reach with a handkerchief, keeping your nose far cleaner," says Dr. Bischinger. "And eating the dry remains of what you pull out is a great way of strengthening the body's immune system...when this mixture arrives in the intestines it works just like a medicine."

Dr. Bischinger did not, however, admit to picking and eating his own boogers.

That may sound gross, but I know a six-year-old who freely acknowledges that she enjoys the taste of snot. Do you? No, you say? OK, then tell me how you know what it tastes like? Got ya there!

Dear Dr. Gross

My family and I live in the country and we always have green boogers. My friend from London, England, e-mailed me the other day and said his boogers are usually black. What gives?

Signed,
Country Nose-Picker

Dear Nose-Picker:

Nasal mucus, snot or boogers as you call them, aren't always green. In fact, booger colors can range from clear to shades of yellow, brown or gray. It all depends on what the mucus has collected. Your friend who lives in the big city is exposed to large amounts of air pollution from industries, cars, trucks and buses. All that black soot goes in the nose and comes out as, well, black snot.

As for the average green snot, most nose mucus contains bacteria and enzymes called peroxidases, which are green and kill that bacteria. Peroxidases make many things green, such as wasabi—the green, toothpaste-like goop often eaten with sushi. Two of the most common bacteria are also found in nasal mucus. One is golden yellow in color and the other is bluish. Mix blue and yellow and what do you get? Green! Green snot is usually normal, but green, brown or yellow phlegm isn't. When you have a respiratory infection, lung mucus or phlegm ("sputum" when it comes up) is often coughed out in globs. Time to see a doctor.

Big ZZZs

Snoring can be irritating...and loud. If your neighbors complain, you've got a serious problem. Air you breathe flows over your airways and causes the tissues there to vibrate just like a musical instrument. It's not, however, music to most people's ears. Men and overweight people snore the most. Sleep apnea is a more serious problem. People actually stop breathing for a short time, which causes them to wake up, and they don't get a good night's rest. They may need to wear special devices when they sleep or may require surgery.

Just be glad you're not a neighbor of Melvin Switzer. This British dockworker holds the world record as the loudest snorer. How loud? Eighty-eight decibels (or "dB," but more on that in the next section). That's about the same intensity as a Harley-Davidson motorcycle engine revving up beside your bed. Mrs. Switzer put up with it, though she's now deaf in one ear.

EARS to YOU

Some people love their ears; some people hate them. They can be too big, stick out too much or have repulsive ear hairs. But if you're lucky, they look just right. Some people dress them up with a simple pair of earrings, a curvy row of six or a big, stretched hole that never gets smaller unless they pay a surgeon to fix it. Ears may not be the prettiest part of the human body, but they are useful!

A Nod to Mr. Spock

The outer ear, or pinna, has ridges and folds made of cartilage, whereas the earlobe is soft. Ears contain relatively few blood vessels but still have sensitive nerve endings, so if you pinch, pierce or let your dog lick them, you'll definitely wince. And that pointy little flap on the front of your outer ear? That's the tragus. It's fun to play with it when you're bored in class, and along with the pinna, likely helps to channel sound waves into your ear canal.

Once sound waves are collected from outside the ear, they move down the ear canal to the eardrum, or tympanic membrane, which is like the skin on a drum. Touch it, and it starts to vibrate. As the eardrum vibrates, it makes the hammer, anvil and stirrup move, too. Those are actually the common names of the three teeny, tiny bones in your middle ear—the malleus, incus and stapes.

The inner ear contains semicircular canals and a snail-shaped organ called the cochlea, both of which are filled with a watery fluid. Inside the cochlea is the organ of Corti, where hair cells covered in tiny cilia detect different vibrations. Cilia send their messages via nerves to your brain until bam—you've just heard a sound!

Hear Ye, Hear Ye

Sound intensities are measured in decibels, or dB. When your mom politely tells you to clean your room, she's speaking at a volume around 60 dB. If you crank up the music so that you can't hear her anymore, you're probably subjecting your ears to 100 dB. Sit in the front row of a rock concert and you're at 110 dB. Listening to that level of sound for long periods of time can damage your hearing. If you get bored and go outside to light firecrackers with your friend, you're exposed to about 120 dB.

The Roar of the Crowd

Loud, prolonged noises, such as those over 85 dB, hurt the cilia and may cause hearing damage. Be careful if you attend hockey playoffs. Researchers studying the effects of crowd noise at hockey games found that it can potentially harm your hearing. During game three of the 2006 NHL Stanley Cup playoff series between the Carolina Hurricanes and the Edmonton Oilers, the noise level hit 93 dB during the intermissions. When a goal was scored, it shot up to over 120 dB.

For the three hours, the average noise level was about 104 dB, or the same as listening to a running chainsaw an arm's length away. Most people at the game probably recovered their hearing after a day or so, but if they had been in a workplace or factory, by law they would have needed hearing protection.

Did You Hear That?

Your ears get bigger as you get older. They grow a miniscule amount every year, but you don't have to worry about looking like Dumbo the Elephant unless you live thousands of years.

AGE
10

AGE
13

AGE
20

AGE
31

Ear Bugs

You had a wonderful time at the beach, jumping into the waves and snorkeling. You brought back pebbles, seashells— and a bad itch inside your ear that's driving you crazy. You've got otitis externa, or swimmer's ear. It occurs when there is too much moisture in the ear from bathing, showering, swimming or, for some people, wearing a hearing aid. You can even get it from those popular tiny earphones that go with MP3 players.

What happens is that bacteria overgrow in the ear and it gets itchy. If it's really bad, you've got an itchy infection. It might look stupid, but blow-drying your ears helps remove water from the inside of your ears. Over-the-counter ear drops can also help kill the bacteria. Just remember, don't swab out your earwax. Your ears need it for protection, and besides, you'll only push the wax in farther.

Potatoes in Your Ears

Earwax. It's one of those things you don't think about until a friend tells you there's a clump of gunk sticking out of your ear. Or you shove a finger into your ear canal, probe around, then pull it out and say, "Yuck!"

Earwax, also known as cerumen, works to keep the eardrum water resistant and supple. It's not made by miniature bumble bees in your ear but, rather, is secreted by the ceruminous glands (special sebaceous, or oil-producing, glands), which constantly churn out the waxy stuff.

By slowly moving down the ear canal to the outside (at about the same rate as your fingernails grow), cerumen sweeps away dead cells, dust and anything else that may have settled inside your ear. The wax also helps prevent the skin inside your ear canal from becoming one itchy tube by lubricating it and reducing the amount of certain bacteria and fungi.

If you want to help keep that wax conveyer belt working, simply move your jaw more. Opening and closing the jaw slightly shifts the ear canal, shaking up the gunk and helping the earwax chug along. This gives you another good reason to yak away on the phone or chew on a huge wad of gum.

The Wet or Dry Gunk

You might think everyone's earwax looks the same. Wrong. If you're of Caucasian or African heritage, you've probably got the yellow-brown, sticky or "wet" type of earwax. Asians and Native Americans have gray and flaky "dry" earwax. It's all in the genes, though the wet type is dominant.

As people get older, their earwax tends to get drier, and it flows less easily out of the ear. Their ears can get plugged to the point where they can't hear well. Poking a cotton swab or finger into the ear canal merely compacts the stuff. It's better to soften the earwax with oil or get a doctor to flush out the ear canal with water. You'll be amazed at all the chunks floating in the water afterwards!

Earwax Trivia

During the Middle Ages, people must have been just as obsessed with earwax as we are today. Monks were known to have added earwax to the pigments they used for illuminated manuscripts. And for those with earaches, a common cure was to drop the fat of a warm, freshly killed hen into the ear canal. This remedy probably worked because fat is oily, and any oil will help break up hardened earwax (too bad for the hen!).

Googly Eyes

Get out a mirror and peer deep into your eyes. Don't they look freaky? See that black dot that gets bigger or smaller depending on how much light you shine into it? It's really just a hole. A hole in your eye! See that colored part around it? Those are simply muscle fibers. And the whites of your eyes? They're filled with a jelly-like goo.

Yep, your eyes don't look so lovely when you check out each part. What's more is that when you look at your eyes or those of another person, you are only seeing about 20 percent of each eye. The rest is hidden in that dip within the skull called the eye socket. If our eyes weren't held by eye sockets, we'd all look like googly-eyed bugs!

Let the Light In

Your eyes are just like a camera in your head, a jelly-ball camera that is. That hole, the pupil, controls how much light enters your eye. In brightly lit places, such as a classroom or outside in the sunshine, the pupil gets smaller and allows only some light to enter. If it didn't, you'd literally be blinded by the light! In dimly lit environments, such as a darkened bedroom or movie theater, the pupil gets larger, or dilates. The pupil lets in as much light as it can so your eye can see what's going on around you.

How does the pupil change size? That's the job of the iris, those colored muscle fibers that surround the pupil. The word "iris" comes from the Greek goddess of the rainbow whose name was, surprise, Iris. I have yet to see someone (who wasn't wearing contact lenses) with indigo or yellow eyes, but there are a lot of eye colors out there. You may have blue eyes, your cousin has green eyes and your weird friend has one blue and one brown eye.

The color of your iris comes from a pigment called melanin, which is also found in your skin. If you have a lot of this pigment in your iris, you have brown eyes. Smaller amounts make the iris appear blue, gray or green.

Windows to the World

Light rays entering the eye first hit a transparent, dome-shaped "window" called the cornea. This is the place where the light rays get bent, so to speak, and continue through a clear, thick, watery fluid called the aqueous humor.

Light is then focused by the lens, a clear, elastic disk. The lens in your eye is not much different than the lens on a camera. You have one lens in each eye, unless you are a dragonfly—it has about 30,000 lenses in each eye!

You can compare your eye lens to an onion, with 22,000 transparent layers of long cells called lens fibers. These fibers also make the lens stretchy so it can change shape. After the light goes through the lens, it passes through a firm gel called the vitreous humor until it reaches the retina, a layer of special cells at the back of the eye that work like a movie screen.

Sore Sclera

Sclera is the name for the whites of your eyes. It's a tough covering that protects your eye, but the tissues below it can show through. Older people have yellow-looking sclera, and in young children, it almost looks bluish. Infections, smoke, chlorine from a swimming pool, rubbing your eyes or staying up late can make the blood vessels underneath the sclera swell. The next thing you know, you've got sore, red, bulging veins—bloodshot eyes.

A Topsy-Turvy World

Covering the retina are photosensitive cells that trigger nerve impulses. This information shoots through the optic nerves that come out of the back of each eyeball and continue to the brain. When an image is produced on the retina, it is actually upside down! Fortunately, the brain turns the image right-side up, otherwise we'd all be very confused indeed.

We can see thanks to the rods and the cones in our eyes. No, they don't have anything to do with sticks and ice cream. Rods and cones are photoreceptors, and we have millions of these specialized cells in the retina.

Rods are sensitive to changes in light and movement. Cones work in bright light and help us see colors. People who don't have all their cones can be color-blind. They may not be able to see green or red (which could make Christmastime rather interesting), or blue and yellow. A few people don't see any colors at all, so they see their world in shades of gray, just like you'd see on those old black-and-white TVs.

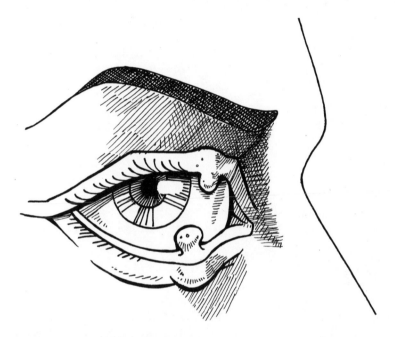

Pigpens and Sties

"Pigpen" is the nickname for the filthy little boy in Charlie Brown cartoons who is always surrounded by a cloud of dirt. If anyone were prone to eye sties, it would be Pigpen! A sty (or stye) is an aggravating bump along your eyelash line. Eyelashes are good at trapping dust and germs, but when the tiny glands at their base get infected, they swell up and become a sty. It honestly has nothing to do with a pig's living quarters—a pig sty—though both are rather unappealing.

Floaters

It's a beautiful day in the park. You're lying on the grass, gazing up at the big, beautiful blue sky. You see birds, a plane and, hey, what's that? A strange, shapeless object moves slowly across your eye, then disappears. It seemed to be "in" your eye!

Well, it was. What you saw was the shadow of a floater, usually a piece of a blood vessel or other particle stuck in the jelly-like vitreous humor. Floaters are destined to forever drift around in the eye. Sorry, you can't flush them away like the other, very different kind of floater your body produces.

Oozing Eye

Stay away from people with conjunctivitis, or pinkeye. That's a contagious eye infection of the conjunctiva, a thin membrane that covers the eye. It can be caused by bacteria or a virus. Your eyes become sore and red (or pink), and a thick,

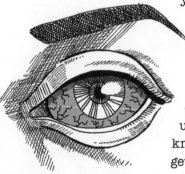

yellow or whitish goo oozes out of the corners of your eyes. It's full of the dead, white blood cells that are there to fight the infection. You wake up with really crusty, stuck-together eyes. Pinkeye is terribly unattractive, and everyone knows it's infectious, so they won't get too close.

Seeing Stars

BOINK! You just banged your head on a low doorway. Did you see stars and colors? Well, then you just saw phosphenes. You can also get them by rubbing your eyes or squeezing them shut. Either way, you've stimulated the nerves enough to produce specks of light that seem to zoom around under your eyelids like mini-UFOs!

Staring Contest

You have a blind spot. Everyone does. It's that part of the retina that doesn't contain any photoreceptors. Want to "see" it? Try this little experiment:

Below is a black "x" on the far left, and a black "o" on the far right. Hold this page about an arm's length away from your face. Close your left eye. Look at the "x" with your right eye. Slowly bring this page closer to your face. Eventually, the "o" disappears! That happens when the "o" falls within your blind spot. You can do the reverse, too. Close your right eye and stare at the "o." See (or rather don't see), you have a blind spot!

𝕏   ọ

When you stare at an object, say, a freshly baked apple pie, your eyes are still moving, even though they appear to be fixated. These eye movements are very fast and small;

you can't even tell you are making them. If your eyes didn't move, the pie picture would fade away. The neurons in your eyes and brain think "oh, nothing there" and stop sending out information. The pie picture would fade away. No pie in the eye, no dessert for you.

Anyone Seen My Eye?

Can your eyeball fall out? It's rare, but it can happen. In 2006, NCAA basketball player Allan Ray's eyeball seemed to pop out of its socket when another player accidentally hit him. Dazed and unable to see, Ray was helped off the court while a medic held a gloved hand over Ray's eyes to prevent the situation from worsening and, well, also because it was a rather gross sight.

There is an actual condition called a globe luxation. When it happens, the eyeball can be gently pushed back into place, and eyesight eventually returns, unless there's been damage to the optic nerve or the muscles around the eye. Some people can intentionally pop out their eyeballs, whereas others find that this occurs when they push their eyes or insert contact lenses. Then there's what happens when you have a big sneeze, just like in the cartoons: Your eyes literally pop out of your head.

DiD YOU KNOW?

Your eyeballs stop growing when you're about seven or eight years old.

Liquidy Layers

There's a coating covering your eyeball—a thin tear film. Contact lenses float on this tear film, which is made of three layers. The top one, the lipid layer, is oily and super skinny. It's made by special glands in the eyelid that ensure your eyes don't dry out. Under that is the thick aqueous layer, which is sometimes called the lacrimal layer. "Aqueous" means "water," and this layer provides oxygen for your eyes. Your eyes need oxygen. They sure do. Eyes without oxygen are dry, itchy and very irritated.

The last layer of the tear film is called the mucin layer. It's made by goblet cells that lie right on the eyeball's surface. The mucin layer is a slimy glue that keeps the tear film stuck to the eye where it's supposed to be.

Enter Sandman

When you blink, you coat your eyes with mucin, an antibacterial protein, which keeps them moist and healthy. Most people blink about 15 times a minute, or about 14,400 times a day (not including sleep time). When you sleep, it's a different story. There usually isn't enough mucin swishing around all night to dissolve the tears that sometimes collect in the corners of your eyes. These tears get pushed out and collect into little clumps that dry on the skin just outside the eye. The term for this is "hardened rheum," also called sleepers, sandman, crusties or eye boogers. The Japanese language actually refers to these dry clumps as "eye crap."

My Eyes Are Leaking

Tears are mostly water, but they also contain some mucin and small amounts of other ingredients, including sodium (or salt), which gives them a salty taste. They're made by glands in your eyelids called lacrimal glands. Tears are great at washing away tiny particles of dust, dirt and dead skin cells, keeping the eye in tip-top shape with a constant watery bath.

Most people blink about 15 times a minute, or about 14,400 times a day (not including sleep time).

Some people can even **blow air bubbles** from their eyes underwater.

Eye-Blowing Bubbles

Tears also wash into the nose via the nasolacrimal ducts. Some people can even blow air bubbles from their eyes underwater. Here's an interview with Kenneth Keith Kallenbach, a 37-year-old actor from Pennsylvania who can blow air bubbles through his eyes.

Q: When did you first discover you could blow bubbles through your eyes?

Ken: I always knew I could blow air through my eyes as a little kid. When I was 14 or 15 I would go to parties and blow cigarette smoke through my eyes in front of people. It used to be a steady stream, but now I can't do it as well. It also burns my eyes badly and I don't like smoking.

Q: When bubbles come out of your eyes, do they come out of your ears, too?

Ken: No, just out of my eyes, but I have heard of someone who can blow smoke out of his ears.

Q: How do you blow air bubbles through your eyes underwater?

Ken: I have to hold my nose and blow. To do it underwater, I wear a snorkeling mask filled with water and blow. I used to be able to do it through both eyes but now I usually just do it through one.

Q: Have you done this in front of an audience?

Ken: Yes, in 1990, I got on the Howard Stern show. On October 7, 2005, I was on the Jay Leno show. I've been a regular on the Howard Stern show, too. I also have a new DVD out about me through my website, www.kennethkeith.com

I SEE!

If you wear eyeglasses, eating carrots won't improve your eyesight. You'll still need the glasses, but carrots do contain beta-carotene and nutrients, which keep your eyes healthy.

Monster MOUTH

You wake up in the morning feeling positively gross. OK, who hasn't? Your breath stinks. You've got crusty stuff in the corners of your eyes. Your skin feels greasy and smells like you haven't bathed (which you haven't). You need a shower badly. Yep, these are the "Monster Mornings." The human body can be pretty gross, huh?

Dear Dr. Gross

I share a room with my brother and he's always up before me. But this morning, it wasn't his yelling that woke me up—it was his bad breath! He was three feet away from me, but I could still smell it. It stunk so bad, I thought I was going to die! Why was his breath so stinky?

Signed,
Half-Dead in the Morning

Dear Half-Dead:

Blame it on bacteria. They are the cause of your brother's bad breath. We scientists call it halitosis. You probably had it this morning. too. It's especially nasty first thing in the morning, because your mouth has probably been pretty dry most of the night (you produce less saliva while asleep). Even if you drooled on your pillow in your sleep, it didn't stay in your mouth. Oxygen and enzymes in saliva keep bacteria at a good balance, so lots of saliva means less bad breath (all the more reason to chew sugarless gum!).

The Road to Bad Breath

1st Stop

Food particles remain in the mouth long after you have swallowed your last bite of dinner.

2nd Stop

There are over 500 types of bacteria hiding in the nooks and crannies of your mouth, and they love to eat those bits of leftover food.

3rd Stop

After their dinner, the bacteria in the mouth excrete volatile sulfur compounds (VSCs).

4th Stop

You talk to someone. They gag and keel over!

Ways to Prevent Bad Breath

1. Brush your teeth.
2. Brush your tongue, especially the back of it.
3. Get regular dental checkups.
4. Keep your mouth moist with gum or sips of water.
5. Chew on bits of parsley.

The Bad-Breath Detector

You've heard of the breathalyzer, a machine that police ask a suspected drunk driver to breathe into. A Halimeter is a similar device that was invented in the early 1990s to detect bad breath. You breathe into a tube, and it measures the levels of sulfides (hydrogen sulfide and methyl mercaptan—the VSCs) in your breath. If you don't want to use a Halimeter, you can always ask a trusted friend, or a four-year-old kid. Both will probably give you an honest answer.

A Halimeter is a similar device that was invented in the early 1990s to detect bad breath.

Something Smells Fishy

Once upon a time, according to an ancient Sanskrit text, there was a maiden who stank of rotten fish. Although she couldn't help it that she had body odor, nobody would come near her. She lived a lonely life until a kind god divinely cured her. Is this a true story? No one knows, but there actually is a condition called trimethylaminuria, or fish-odor syndrome. People who suffer from it smell as if they have a decayed fish under their clothes. Our bodies often contain the chemical compound trimethylamine, but most of us also produce the enzyme that neutralizes it. Like her stinky modern counterparts, the poor maiden in the story probably didn't have enough of the enzyme.

CHEW ON This

Babies, five-year-olds, grandpas and hockey players: we expect them to be missing their chompers. The rest of us, however, would look a bit scary without teeth. Not only that, but it's also hard to eat a meal without a mouthful of them. The sharp incisor teeth in the front of your mouth are great at cutting and tearing food. The short, flat ones at the back, the molars, chew and mash food into a pulp. Two-thirds of our teeth—the roots—are out of sight, and they're anchored into the gums and jaw by cementum, which, as its name suggests, works like cement.

Plaque Attack

Ever scrape a fingernail over one of your back teeth? See that whitish, sticky film? It's plaque and is full of live, and dead, bacteria. Yuck! Plaque builds up on your teeth, eats away at the enamel and starts to harden. After two weeks, it's so hard we call it tartar, or calculus (nothing to do with math class).

Plaque can make your teeth smell. It can also lead to gum problems, such as gingivitis and periodontal disease. If left on your tooth too long, it will create a hole—a cavity.

You'll have to go to the dentist to get the cavity filled, or the tooth could fall out.

Baby teeth are replaced by permanent teeth, and once they go, they're gone for good. To get rid of plaque, you have to brush and floss at least twice a day and see your dentist regularly. Dentists can get rid of the tartar that you can't remove effectively at home. Or you could follow one old wives' tale and rub baby teeth with the brain of a rabbit to prevent plaque, though I don't think dentists recommend it. Besides, minty toothpaste is much more pleasant.

A Lime a Day Keeps Disease Away

Vitamin C is important for healthy gums. Historically, explorers who were stuck on ships for months on end often didn't have access to fresh fruits and vegetables. Their gums became sore and full of holes. They lost their teeth and got ugly spots all over their skin. Eventually, British ship captains realized that if the sailors sucked on limes, rich in vitamin C, throughout their voyages, they didn't develop gum disease and scurvy. And that's how we got the term "limey" to describe the British!

Old-Fashioned Toothpicks

OK, you've probably seen people pick their noses, but what about picking teeth? It happens, a lot, and it's almost as gross as watching them pick their noses and eat the contents. Except that when you pick your teeth, the gunk is already in your mouth! It usually appears after meals. Bits of food, such as spinach and seeds, get stuck between your teeth. You could use dental floss or a toothpick to get them out, but who has those on hand (no pun intended)? Picking at a tooth with your finger may be impolite, but it's, well, handier.

Shades of Yellow

When was the last time you saw a movie star with yellow teeth? About the last time you saw a pig fly, right? Everybody wants pearly whites. Nobody likes yellowish teeth, unless you're a vampire or zombie.

The part of the tooth that you can see is the crown. It's covered in the hardest substance in the body, enamel. Enamel protects your teeth from all the biting and chewing you do. It is usually white in color, but some people's teeth are naturally more yellow. Eating, smoking and drinking coffee or tea can stain teeth.

You can buy tooth whiteners to bleach the enamel. However, some of these products tend to make your teeth sensitive. Other whitening agents, such as certain toothpastes, have a gritty texture because they contain abrasives. Using them too much is the same as rubbing sandpaper on your teeth—you'll wear down the enamel until it's very thin. Very acidic drinks, such as colas, can also erode the surface of your teeth. And guess what? The layer underneath might start to show through. That layer is called dentin—and it's typically a yellow or even slightly brownish color.

The Root of the Problem

What do you think most people dread hearing at the dentist's office? Is it, "Here is your bill"? No, that's not it. How about, "You need a root canal"? Right!

A root canal procedure means that a dentist has to drill deep into the canals of a tooth. Bet you didn't know you even **had** canals in your teeth. They are thin tubes with blood vessels and sensitive nerves that connect to the soft tissue in the middle of your tooth, the pulp.

If the pulp gets infected, the dentist has to drill into the tooth and scrape the pulp out of the root canals. Sometimes a root canal is done to save a tooth that has turned gray because of damage. Either way, root canals aren't as painful as they used to be—at least that's what I've been told.

Lumpy Jaw Disease

Back in the old days, people rarely brushed their teeth. Needless to say, few had bright pearly whites. No wonder no one smiled for portraits. Even Queen Elizabeth I of England was missing teeth, and the ones she did have were black.

For most people throughout history, tooth abscesses were a major headache. Cavities or gum disease could easily cause a pocket of pus inside or near the tooth. As the bacteria

A root canal procedure means that a dentist has to drill deep into the canals of a tooth.

grew, so did the infection. It was often called "lumpy jaw" because the whole area would swell up.

Sometimes the bone around the tooth dissolved and the tooth would fall out. And that wasn't always the end of the problem. If the infection spread to other parts of the body, such as the blood or brain, it could kill you.

Grind and Bear It

If you wake up with a sore jaw, chips or flattened parts on your teeth, you might have bruxism, or a tooth-grinding problem. This is not the tooth clenching we do when we're angry, but the unconscious kind that usually happens when we're asleep. About 15 to 20 percent of people have a real problem with bruxism. It can be so bad that it even breaks a tooth. A plastic mouth guard worn during sleep protects the teeth from the grinding. And if you wear it with a helmet and pair of skates to bed, you may dream that you're in the NHL.

Sticking it OUT

Good ol' Mr. Tongue. He's not the prettiest bundle of muscles in the body (OK, so which ones are?), but he sure is one of the most useful. Still, he gets no respect. Teachers don't want to see him, but if you are sick, doctors do. He helps us taste, chew, swallow and talk, but most people keep him hidden in their mouths. And if you happen to stick Mr. Tongue out in front of your teacher, just say you wanted to explain these things:

- Parts of the tongue include the tip, blade, body and root.

- You can't swallow your tongue because deep down, it's attached to bone.

- The small bumps on your tongue are papillae, and most contain taste buds.

- You have over 9000 taste buds in your mouth.

- You also have taste buds on your pharynx, palate and larynx.

- Each taste bud only lives for about 10 days.

- People over 60 have usually lost half their taste buds.

Unfortunately, if your teacher is 60 years old, you'll probably get sent to the office for that last comment. Either that, or you'll be told to bite your tongue. At least you've still got most of your taste buds.

Tongue Fun

Next time you eat something, pause a moment and think of Mr. Tongue's job. He pushes food around in your mouth so that your teeth can tear and chew it. He rolls the food around into a ball shape, called a bolus. Then Mr. Tongue helps push the food to the back of your mouth so it can slide down your throat.

The Tongue Print

Everyone knows we all have unique fingerprints. Unless we have an identical twin, our fingerprints are one of a kind. But did you also know that people have a distinct tongue print? It's true. The way the papillae are ordered on your tongue is as individual as you are.

So why aren't people identified by their tongue prints? Just imagine

what would happen down at the precinct. "Ma'am, I'll need your tongue print for identification purposes. First, let me dry your tongue, otherwise the ink wipes right off. "

Tongue Tricks

Can you roll your tongue into a "U" or "W" shape? Not everyone can, but 85 percent of people can curl their tongues into a tube shape. At one time, it was thought to be a hereditary trait. The tongue is super bendable and can move in many directions. It can dart, flick, flap, wag and wiggle, and it also helps us whistle, blow bubbles and catch snowflakes. And when you get older and want to kiss someone, well, let's just say that Mr. Tongue is happiest when he finds a friend.

Cranky Cankers

Those little ulcers, or open sores, that appear in your mouth are canker sores. They are often red, inflamed spots and sometimes have a yellowish center. No one really knows why some people are more prone to canker sores than others. It can be from certain foods, your toothpaste or brushing habits, or emotional stress. They usually heal within a few weeks, but in the meantime, they hurt! So yes, you can blame your canker sore for your crankiness.

Dear Dr. Gross

Last week, I scarfed down a bag of candy. The next day, my mom asked me where the candy was. I told her that the dog ate it. A few days later, I got these little, white, painful spots on my tongue. My mom says they are "lie bumps." What happened?

Signed,
Zits On My Tongue

Dear Zits:

You developed transient lingual papillitis, or swollen taste buds, that's what happened. Telling fibs doesn't cause them, but irritation or a small infection can. You can also get swollen taste buds from eating too many candies or sugary snacks. They usually go away on their own in a week or so. In the meantime, keep your mouth as clean as you can, and try not to lie!

other Bumps and Lumps

Since your tongue is good at feeling its way around the inside of your mouth, you may have noticed some strange bumps here and there. You many even have a torus on the roof of your mouth or inside your jaw. It can be small or big, and it doesn't move, but is just a hard growth out of the bone that is covered in gum tissue.

You can also get similar lumps on the outside of your teeth, under the gum. If the salivary ducts in your mouth become sore or filled up, they can cause little blisters. You can even develop the occasional misplaced sebaceous gland here and there. It pops up as a yellow spot on the lining inside your mouth.

Something's Growing on My Mouth

You can feel it coming on. You hope nobody sees it 'cause it looks gross. Cold sores, or herpes simplex, are contagious, so

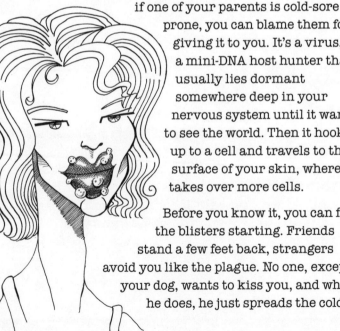

if one of your parents is cold-sore prone, you can blame them for giving it to you. It's a virus, a mini-DNA host hunter that usually lies dormant somewhere deep in your nervous system until it wants to see the world. Then it hooks up to a cell and travels to the surface of your skin, where it takes over more cells.

Before you know it, you can feel the blisters starting. Friends stand a few feet back, strangers avoid you like the plague. No one, except your dog, wants to kiss you, and when he does, he just spreads the cold sore around your mouth. Stressful events seem to cause flare-ups. Keep the blister dry and don't pick it. Also change your toothbrush and toothpaste because the virus can live on them for a long time.

Sandpaper Lips

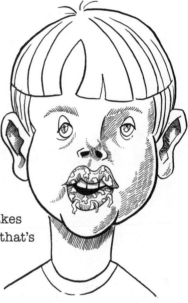

Nobody wants to kiss chapped lips. They are dry, sore and reddish, and they peel. Cold weather makes them 10 times as bad. Putting sunscreen, lip balm or a dab of petroleum jelly on your lips each night can help, as does drinking water. In rare cases, chapped lips can be a sign of a vitamin deficiency. Licking your lips makes it worse. Kids often do this and that's why they get a ring of redness around their lips. So don't lick your lips unless you've just had a delicious meal!

One other thing—the dry, red, scaly skin some people get on the corners of their lips is not the same as a cold sore or chapped lips. It is actually a type of yeast infection. Don't lick those crusty corners either. That will just make it worse!

EWWW!

Your nasal passages, mouth and throat are all interconnected. Some people can suck spaghetti through their nose and out their mouth, then slide it back and forth through the nose and throat.

GOB: More than a SPITFUL

Imagine a whole swimming pool full of spit. Would you want to swim in that? Your average pool holds about 10,000 gallons of water—and that's how much saliva most people produce in a lifetime. Saliva is 98 percent water, so if you had a saliva-filled pool, you could swim in it. It might be too frothy, though.

Where does all this spit come from? Three salivary glands located in the jaw, below your ears and under the tongue constantly produce that watery mouth liquid. It trickles out twice as fast during the day as it does at night. In 24 hours, you could collect about a soda can full of spit. At certain times, such as when you feel as though you might throw up (more on that later), your salivary glands step up production and the spit begins to flow out, sort of like a mini Niagara Falls. And unless you spit it out on the sidewalk (or elsewhere) it gets swallowed.

Besides its usefulness when it comes to licking stamps or sealing envelopes, saliva has other benefits. It keeps the mouth moist and softens food so it can easily go down your throat. Saliva is the first part of digestion. Among other compounds, it contains enzymes that break down carbohydrates in food. You swallow about 295 times during a big dinner, so without saliva, eating meals would be very difficult, indeed.

There may also be a natural painkiller in human saliva. French researchers call the compound they discovered "opiorphin." It works like morphine, another painkiller, but may be even more powerful. And who says licking a wound doesn't make it feel better!

Thin Is In

For spit, that is. Saliva is loaded with bacteria, but swishing it around in your mouth (such as when you chew sugarless gum) can protect your teeth from plaque. And if your salivary glands produce thinner rather than the thicker kind of saliva, you will probably have fewer cavities as well. Researchers think that thinner saliva contains more calcium and is more effective at washing away bacteria and plaque on the teeth. The thicker kind is tackier, almost the consistency of strands of slime, and looks much gunkier, too.

Science of Spit

Saliva, like sweat, pee or most fluids in our body, contains many of the chemicals and medications we ingest. It also contains our very own DNA. Police have been known to collect saliva from the top of a soda can, analyze it and trace it back to a criminal. So if you break the law, then take a swig out of a soda can, watch out where you throw it. The police might be watching—and nail you for more than just littering!

In 24 hours, you could collect about a soda can full of spit.

Burps and BELCHES

Remember the word "onomatopeia" from English class? It means that a word sounds the way it's pronounced. "Burp" is a great example. Even "belch" comes close. The medical term, however—eructation—somewhat misses the boat, though I have heard some burps that start with a long "eeerrrr" sound.

A burp is gas that comes back up and out your mouth. How does the gas get in you? It starts with swallowing air, or aerophagia. Whenever you eat, talk, open your mouth, or yawn, you swallow air. Even your spit (saliva) has tiny air bubbles in it. When you are nervous, you might unconsciously gulp air as well. Drinking fizzy soda pop, which is loaded with carbon dioxide, will also dump gas into your stomach. In that case, the burp is a gassy one, full of carbon dioxide.

Most other burps, though, are usually oxygen and nitrogen. Once in a while, you might smell a really stinky burp. This type of burp contains tiny molecules of whatever you ate, most of which is still in your stomach. Those molecules, whether they are from cabbage rolls or sausage on a bun, bond to the gas and come up with the burp. It's the same as tasting your dinner all over again.

Baby Burps

Babies take in a lot of air when they suck on a bottle or are breastfed. Fortunately, they don't have a problem burping in public. Parents even encourage it. If the gas stays in a baby's stomach, it might cause pain, so after feeding, the baby is patted on the back until he or she lets one rip. Babies' stomach valves aren't very big, though, and once in a while, the burp is full of "spit-up"—milk that comes back up. That's why smart parents keep a "burping cloth" handy, to put under the baby's chin.

once in a while, you might smell a really stinky burp.

To Belch or Not to Belch

In some cultures, a burp means you've had a tasty meal. In Western society, we tend to think of burping as impolite, though most kids, and more than a few grown-ups, can't help but laugh when they hear a burp. People who can burp the alphabet often draw attention in a crowd. You can even listen to other people's burps recorded on the Internet. There's an old expression that says, "It's better to belch and bear the shame, then squelch the belch and bear the pain." How true!

Burping 101

Some people try super hard to burp, but it just doesn't come out. It all depends on your windpipe. Stretchy, longer ones are like a good balloon neck. You fill your windpipe with gas (that is, take in a big gulp of air or a huge swig of soda pop) and let it escape. Each burp is different, no two are alike.

The pitch and length of a burp depends on how air travels through the valve between your stomach and esophagus—the esophageal sphincter. This valve releases the air, either slowly or in one big rush. It's similar to the way air is let out of a tire or through the neck of a balloon. The sphincter vibrates when air passes over it. How slowly or quickly the air escapes depends on the pressure and speed of the air. Burps can be short and perky, or loud and deep, and can last several seconds.

Another sphincter in your body lets air out from the other end (the fart, of course), but we'll let that pass for now.

Danger: Livestock Burping!

You're doing your part to reduce global warming. You take public transit. You recycle plastic bottles and newspapers. You ride a bike. You carpool. You tell cows and sheep to hold in their burps. Say what?

It's true. The burps (and farts) of sheep, cows, horses, llamas and similar animals contain methane. Like the carbon dioxide from our cars, methane heats up the atmosphere and contributes to global warming. The average cow produces about 200 pounds of methane a year. How do we know that? Because researchers actually hooked up tubes to the faces of cows and measured the burps. The results were scary. With more livestock on the planet than ever before, it is estimated that domestic livestock produce about 15 percent of the methane emissions around the world. It might not be practical to eliminate their "burps," but what they eat can make a difference. Some countries have started to give their animals special feed that helps them feel less gassy.

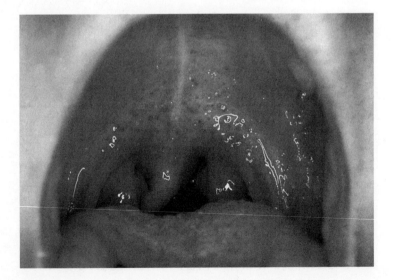

Dear Dr. Gross

I screamed at my sister the other day and she said she could see a funny ugly thing hanging down at the back of my throat? I looked in the mirror and, sure enough, there it was. What is it?

Signed,
Ugly Throat

Dear Ugly Throat:

That would be your uvula. It helps stop food and liquid from pushing up through your nose. Some people who snore too much get their uvula removed.

Another body part that helps food go the right way is the epiglottis, a flap of cartilage in the shape of a leaf. Its main job is to protect the glottis, the opening at the top of your air passage. The epiglottis is actually part of your larynx (or vocal box) and is covered in a slimy mucous membrane to help keep out bits of dirt and dust. Whenever you swallow, your epiglottis automatically folds down over the opening of your windpipe (also called the trachea). If food or liquid got down your windpipe, your body would try to cough it up to keep it from getting into your lungs. Oh, and don't worry that your sister thinks your uvula is ugly. Hers is, too.

Help...I've got the hic... HICCUPS!

Some people call a "hiccup" a "hiccough." Either way, it sounds like a "hic!" repeated over and over again. Strangely enough, the medical term for hiccups is singultus, which makes no sense, because hardly anyone has just a single hiccup.

Hiccups occur when your diaphragm, the large muscle in the lower part of your chest that helps pull air into your lungs, goes crazy. Spicy food, cold drinks, laughing, coughing, or seemingly nothing at all, can irritate the diaphragm and make it spasm. That causes you to gulp air, and the epiglottis quickly slams shut. As the air passes over your voice box, it makes a "hiccup" sound. Now here's a thought: What if you hiccupped and burped at the same time? What would you call that sound explosion? A hicurp or a burcup?

Fishy Hiccups

What is the purpose of a hiccup? No one knows for sure. Babies hiccup in the womb, so the action could be exercise for their underdeveloped breathing muscles. Researchers think hiccups might be linked to another baby trait—sucking. When animals suck, the glottis gets covered the same way it does during a hiccup. The ancient ancestors of mammals evolved from the sea and had gills. Interestingly, a primitive air breather, such as a lungfish or tadpole, covers its glottis when water goes over its gills. Therefore, the hiccup could be a leftover primitive reflex from a time when we were swimming happily in the seas!

Scaring the Hiccup outta Ya

On the scale of "socially embarrassing sounds coming out of your body," a hiccup is rather low on the list. Still, hiccups can be very annoying.

BOO

Hic !...

Once they start, it's hard to make them stop. Hiccup home remedies include (but are not limited to):

- breathing into a bag
- drinking water while upside down
- drinking water while plugging your ears
- eating peanut butter
- eating sugar
- scaring someone
- sneezing

Most hiccups usually go away on their own, though certain nerves in the body seem to be connected to hiccups. In serious cases, doctors prescribe medication to help the hiccup sufferer. One researcher found that massaging the rectum—yep, that part where poop comes out—quickly stopped hiccups. Hey, at least he discovered a drug-free cure!

DiD YOU KNOW?

Charles Osborne of Anthon, Iowa, had a hiccup bout that lasted from 1922 to 1990! I wonder how many times people snuck up behind him and tried to scare him out of the hiccups.

A Chestful of Balloons

Your lungs are like two spongy balloons in your chest. Every time you breathe in, they expand. Breathe out and they get smaller. Your lungs' goal is to get oxygen from the air into your body and to push carbon dioxide back out.

They do this with the help of zillions of tiny little balloons called alveoli. These air sacs have thin, elastic walls, and on the inside surface, you often find some special white blood cells. They're waiting there, just ready to pounce on any germs brought in from the air.

Have Cold, Will Travel

You might think that because air is invisible, there is nothing in it, but air has billions of bugs. Germs, viruses, bacteria, fungi—you name it. When some of these bugs get into the air passages that lead to our lungs, they multiply and cause respiratory infections. The common cold is one of them. Colds are caused by a virus, and there are about 200 of these cold-causing viruses around. It's not hard to catch a cold because viruses usually stick around until they find a "host." Here's an example of how this happens:

Person A has a cold. He sneezes and the virus gets carried in the sneeze droplets. They land on the floor, his chair, his desk and his hands— everywhere around him!

Person A then shakes hands with Person B. Person B has no idea that she just picked up the cold virus. After lunch, Person B picks a piece of spinach out of her teeth. The virus travels from her hand to the mucous membranes in her mouth. It keeps multiplying and gets into her bloodstream. To fight off this new infection, Person B's blood vessels and mucous membranes in her nose start to swell. All the extra mucus gives her a runny nose and makes her sneeze, and voilá, she's got a cold!

Question: What could Person B have done to prevent catching the cold virus?

Answers:

a) Worn gloves (á la Queen of England)

b) Stayed home from work that day to sit around watching TV or reading

c) Avoided Person A like the plague

d) Washed her hands

e) All of the above

It's not hard to catch a cold because viruses usually stick around until they find a "host."

The correct answer is "e) All of the above," but since we live in the real world, Person B could have done the most practical thing, which is "d) Washed her hands."

Cover your MOUTH!

You're in a room quiet enough to hear a pin drop. If you wait long enough, someone is bound to cough. Cough. Cough. We do it to clear our throat. Sometimes it's a nervous habit, but usually we cough because there is something irritating our windpipe or esophagus.

Like blinking when someone blows in your eyes, coughing is a reflex. If dust or smoke starts to bother the lining of your respiratory passages, you cough. If you are eating and food goes down the wrong way, you cough. If you have a cold and there's a ton of phlegm coming out, you cough. Too much coughing can hurt, and if you have a broken or bruised rib, trying to cough is like getting a tooth pulled—very painful!

There is a certain type of person, however, who loves to cough and sneeze. He or she is a steruphiliac and is very strange indeed.

Cough It Up

Air can shoot up your windpipe faster than a Formula One racer, but once it comes out, it has slowed down to average highway speed. The stuff shooting out of your mouth can be full of viruses, germs, saliva—and sometimes chunks of your most recent sandwich, if they didn't make it properly down into your stomach.

When you cough, your body is trying to get rid of something to prevent it from going into your lungs. Some of the grossest stuff you can cough up is phlegm or sputum. Both are mucus from your respiratory passages, full of bacteria, germs and other foreign particles. Some medicines help suppress dry coughs, whereas others, expectorants, help you cough up all that yucky phlegm, gob and loogie stuff.

Some of the grossest stuff you can cough up is phlegm or sputum.

The Answer Is (cough) B

In April 2003, Charles Ingram of Britain was found guilty of deception, for cheating on the TV show, "Who Wants To Be A Millionaire." Ingram, a retired major in the army, had been on the show two years earlier and won one million pounds. His wife, Diana, and a third accomplice, Tecwen Whittock, were also convicted. Tapes of the show were used in court to prove that Whittock coughed during correct answers. In his defense, Whittock said he suffered from allergies. The jury didn't buy that explanation. Whittock and the Ingrams maintain to this day that they are innocent and were wrongly convicted.

Coughs that Kill

Here lies the beloved John Adam Doe.
Caught consumption, now he's buried below.

It's a sad fact, but throughout history, millions of people have died of killer coughs. Today, we have vaccines against most of them, such as whooping cough. Also called pertussis, this disease often struck young children. Their coughs developed a weird wheezing or "whoop" sound.

Another potentially deadly disease was consumption. People with consumption sometimes coughed so much that they would bring up blood. Other symptoms included fever, aches and loss of appetite, which is why it was called the "wasting disease." Victims seemed to "waste away" before their families' eyes.

We now know that consumption is an infectious lung disease, called tuberculosis (TB). Two million people around the world still die from TB every year. Most live in poor countries and can't afford the antibiotic treatment or the vaccination shots that prevent the disease in the first place.

It's a sad fact, but throughout history, millions of people have died of killer coughs.

A Yawn Is A Big Hole

Are yawns ugly? Face it, nobody asked you to display your bacteria-filled mouth with its gunk-topped teeth, pasty tongue and bits of unchewed food. OK, if yawns are so disgusting, then explain why 55 percent of people who see a yawn actually do the same thing within five minutes?

Yawns have always been a mystery. The ancient Greeks and Mayans thought that a yawn meant your soul was trying to escape and get to heaven. Other cultures believed that yawns might let evil spirits into your body. Animals, humans, even babies in the womb yawn, but we really don't know why.

When the brain triggers a yawn reflex, it could be the body's way of taking in more air because the cells need oxygen. Some think that yawns can be explained by evolution. Since yawning shows the teeth, it may have been a show of dominance or a "don't bother me" gesture. Yawns might also be a way to keep the body at the right temperature. When you yawn, you stretch your mouth and often other parts of your body, thereby improving your blood circulation.

Then again, maybe we yawn because we are just bored and it's something to do. Either way, I think you'll agree that pandiculation (the act of yawning and stretching) might look silly when someone else does it, but when you do it, it sure feels great.

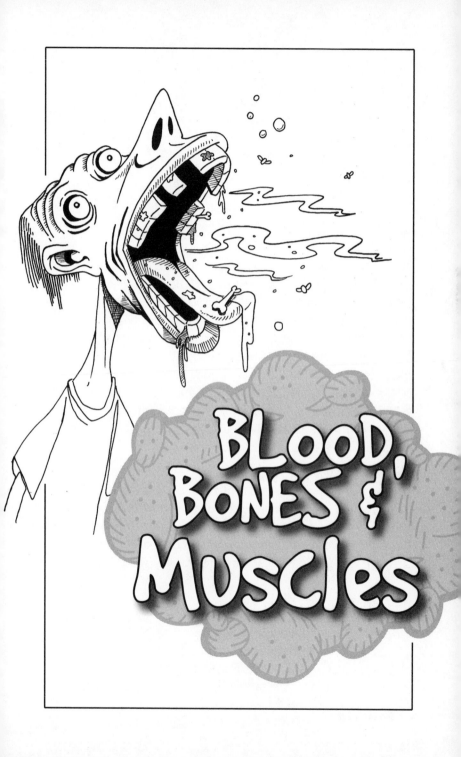

Bloody BASICS

If you're squeamish about blood, cover your eyes the next time Cecil B. DeMille's "The Ten Commandments" is on TV. It's a classic movie that is rerun during the Easter holiday and has a couple of "blood" scenes that I'll never forget. In one, Moses (a.k.a. Charlton Heston) dips his rod into the Nile, instantly creating a swirl of blood. The Pharaoh (a.k.a. Yul Brenner) later tries to clean up the famous Egyptian river. He says a few words and grabs a vase of clear water. As soon as he pours the water into the river, it changes to blood, which makes the situation worse.

Blood. Most of us don't want to see it, but we can't live without it. Lose more than 40 percent of your blood, and you might not survive. Blood is the river of life that runs through our bodies. That river is called the circulatory system, because the blood flows around in the body through vessels, pumped through by the good old-fashioned heart.

That Red Highway

Blood supplies oxygen to our cells, along with nutrients such as glucose, amino acids and fatty acids. It carries a bunch of other goodies, too, such as hormones and special proteins. Blood also takes away wastes from each cell, including carbon dioxide. And it keeps our body warm.

Technically, blood is a tissue. It's a group of similar cells that work together and circulate through our body via the circulatory system. Blood travels through vessels called veins, which take it to the heart, and arteries that carry it

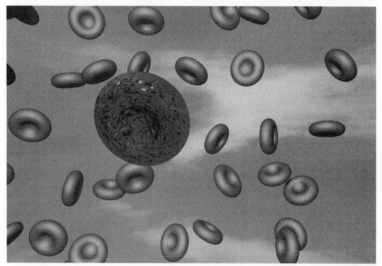

away. Every day, your blood goes on a 60,000 mile journey through your body. Yep, there are enough blood vessels in your body to go around the entire Earth two and a half times! That's one long, red highway.

our Bleeding Past

Ancient cultures knew that blood was important stuff. Many thought it contained the soul or spirit of a person. Blood was associated with sacrifice, and the blood of animals was often offered to the gods. In Imperial Rome, the blood of fallen gladiators was believed to be a medicinal cure. People suffering from epilepsy and other illnesses were actually encouraged to drink it.

For centuries, many people had the crazy idea that certain illnesses were caused by having too much blood in the body. To cure that, they practiced bloodletting, or slicing a bit here and there to let some of the blood out. No wonder people were afraid of physicians!

Bloodletting was based on the ancient concept of the four humors in the body (blood, black bile, yellow bile and phlegm). To remain healthy, your humors had to be balanced. You have probably seen those red and white striped poles outside most barber shops. The red symbolizes blood because, throughout history, people went to barbers (who also performed crude surgery in their spare time) to get a vein cut and drain some blood. Patients would squeeze a stick (represented by the pole) to help fill their arm with blood, and the barber then wrapped a tight cloth, or tourniquet (represented by the white) around it before he started to cut.

Another technique of bloodletting was to use leeches, those wormy creatures found in ponds and lakes. Several of them were put on the skin so that they could suck out the "bad blood" until they were so full they'd eventually fall off. Leeches are so good at what they do that doctors today still find uses for them in medicine.

Heart Plumbing

Know any people who are about 70 years old? Tell them that during their lifetime, they have had approximately 2.5 billion heartbeats, which have pumped about 48 million gallons of blood. Hopefully, this news will not give them a heart attack.

The heart is the muscle that pumps blood along its highway. It beats, on average, about 70 times per minute. The heart beats faster when you're exercising or running after a bus, and less when you're watching TV or napping on the couch.

In case you're wondering, the human heart doesn't resemble anything on a Valentine's Day card. It's about the size of your fist and has four sections, or chambers, that are

divided into right and left—
two atria at the top
and two ventricles
at the bottom. Blood
comes into the heart
by two thick veins
(the inferior and superior
vena cava). It travels into
the right atrium, through
a valve and into the right
ventricle. Then it's pumped back up
through the pulmonary artery, where it
dumps off carbon dioxide and picks up
oxygen from the lungs. It goes back through the
pulmonary vein into the left atrium and ventricle, at which
point it gets pumped back out into the aorta and on to the
rest of the body.

The heart has valves, just like in plumbing, to stop the
blood from backing up. If you have heart problems, though,
you should call a doctor, not a plumber.

Thump, Thump Goes My Pulse

Hold two fingers under your jaw. Feel that repeating little
thump, thump? That's your pulse. It's the blood shooting
through your blood vessels with every contraction, or beat,
of your heart. Your heart is either relaxed and filling with
blood, or is pumping; that is, squeezing blood out. That
pressure could squirt blood 30 feet if it didn't have vessels
to travel through and contain it.

A pulse can also be felt on your wrist or behind your knee,
even in your groin, but the neck pulse is the strongest,
because it contains the carotid artery. This artery is one
of the most important vessels in the body. Cut the carotid
artery, and you could bleed to death within seconds.

off the cuff

Ever had your blood pressure checked? The nurse puts a cuff around your upper arm, pumps it full of air, and then stares at the gauge while you sigh in relief that your blood flow hasn't been permanently cut off.

The nurse is measuring how hard your heart has to pump to get the blood moving. High blood pressure means your heart works much too hard. Low blood pressure means you're likely to faint (not enough blood is getting to the brain), which, ironically, sometimes happens to people who don't like that sphygmomanometer (blood pressure gauge!) anywhere near them.

one Bad cut

During an NHL game in March 1989, Buffalo Sabres goalie Clint Malarchuk's throat was accidentally sliced by another player's skate. Blood instantly flooded the ice around the goal, in front of horrified spectators. Seven fans in the arena fainted and two had heart attacks. Millions of TV viewers caught a glimpse of the accident before the cameras cut away from the view. Malarchuk fully recovered from the injury and was back on the ice two weeks later.

High blood pressure means your heart works much too hard.

Eat Your Marrow

OK, so you know it comes out when you bleed, but how does blood actually get into you? One way is through a blood transfusion, where you lie down and doctors pump someone else's blood through your veins. The other way is to make your own. We do it all the time, in our bones. Inside our bones is a spongy layer—the cancellous bone—and inside that, usually in the long bones, is marrow. It's either yellow or red; yellow marrow stores fat, and the red stuff makes blood cells. As people get older, their marrow tends to look more yellow than red.

As people get older, their marrow tends to look more yellow than red.

The next time your family has a roast for Sunday dinner, check out what's inside the meat bone. That sticky, brown stuff is cooked marrow. It's really quite tasty—I used to love to pick it out with a fork and eat it. It goes well with potatoes drenched in boiled and seasoned meat blood, er, gravy. Try it, you'll like it!

One Incredible Voyage

There's another classic movie, this time a science-fiction one from the 1960s, called "Fantastic Voyage." In it, scientists discover a way to shrink themselves so that they are small enough to travel through a human body. In their microscope submarine capsule, they pass through the blood and see all sorts of body parts.

So if you were tiny enough to swim through a blood vessel, what would you see? Most of the blood would be a watery, yellowish fluid called plasma. Plasma is mainly water, with traces of hormones and proteins. Also floating around in the plasma is a steady stream of red blood cells known as erythrocytes. Red blood cells are flexible bags full of an iron-containing protein that carries oxygen, called hemoglobin.

You'd also be able to see platelets, or thrombocytes, in the blood. Platelets really do look like teeny-tiny dinner plates and play a key role in coagulation (blood clotting). They come from special, large cells in bone marrow called megakaryocytes and only live about 10 days.

Along your journey, you'd also come across the occasional white blood cell, or leukocyte. White blood cells are the hired hit men of the blood army. Their goal is to fight—fight disease. When you get an infection, white blood cells move out of the blood and rush into action. They're bigger than red blood cells and come in different types. White blood cells also help make our favorite, thick, gross-out juice—pus.

Gooey GUNK

Here pus, pus, pus. Too bad no one finds pus a cute and cuddly fluid. It's definitely one of the most underappreciated substances our bodies can produce. Pus, also known as liquor puris—I'm sure you've seen it before— is that yellowish white, creamy gunk that drains out of abscesses and pops out of pustules.

What is pus? Dead white blood cells and, in particular, neutrophils, the most common white blood cells. Neutrophils move into infections and swallow the "bad guys"; that is, the bacteria or other germs. And they do this in the strangest way. They actually stick out a fake foot (called a pseudo-podium) to trip the germs and pull them in, where they are then eaten! The technical term is that they "phagocytize" the germs.

There are thousands of these "fake foot" neutrophils in each quarter teaspoon of blood. Once the neutrophil neutralizes a germ, however, it's game over for that brave little white blood cell. Oodles of dead neutrophils pile up and in turn get eaten by other kinds of white blood cells called macrophages.

So your pus is really all those good-guy cells that come in to fight the germs when you get an infection. Pus, we salute you.

Not So Lovely Lymph

The clear fluid you see oozing out of blisters is lymph. It's mostly plasma with some other nutrients, but it also contains cells that love to clean up, just like the germ-eating macrophages and special white blood cells called lymphocytes. Lymphocytes are germ snipers, and when called to action, they fire antibodies or special "attack and destroy" proteins at germs. These snipers hang out in bean-sized clusters called the lymph nodes.

Have you ever had a really bad sore throat? It hurts to swallow because there are two swollen lumps on either side of your throat. You go to the doctor, who starts tapping two cold fingers under your jaw. This is to done to check for swelling (though you already knew that!). Lymph nodes have a habit of ballooning up when they work overtime. You can find these nodes in many places on the body, especially in the neck, groin and armpits. They are part of the lymphatic system, a web of capillaries, vessels and ducts that wind their way throughout your body just like the circulatory system. It might seem like a separate system, but lymph is actually made by blood and eventually ends up back there.

Loads of Swollen Nodes

Your lymphatic system is a big player in your immune system. When it goes down, so does most of your body's resistance to germs. As with other systems, it can get diseased. One horrible historic disease was the bubonic plague of the Middle Ages. Some plagues directly attacked a victim's bloodstream, but this one began with a flea bite that put a certain bacteria into the lymphatic system.

At its peak between 1347 and 1351, the bubonic plague wiped out a huge chunk of the European population, killing one in four people! An infected person developed ugly bumps, called buboes, on the groin, neck and under the armpits. If the buboes burst and pus drained out, the person had a chance of surviving the plague, but if not, the person usually died within a few days.

A Big Fish Story

Your body is full of fluid; we're all really one big water bag. This fluid is either in our cells, outside them, between them or in our blood. Blood and lymph—in fact, all our bodily fluids—are surprisingly like, get this, seawater! As some say, all life evolved from the sea. The difference is that our plasma has some proteins and other trace substances that you can't find in seawater. Still, as they say, say hello to your ancestor— the fish!

DID YOU KNOW?

Every second, your body makes more than two million new blood cells.

Diplomatic Immunity

Ever had the measles or chicken pox? Usually you only get these diseases once. That's because your body made antibodies to fight these germs when they come around again.

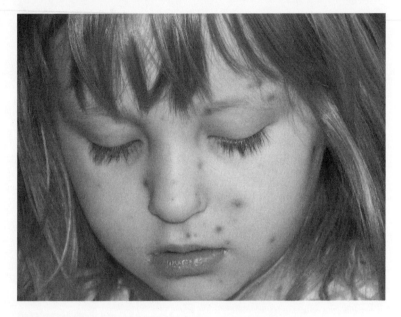

You can build up your immunity naturally or through vaccines. Some vaccines, such as those against polio, can be taken by mouth. But most are injected into your body by a grumpy, busy nurse who seems to enjoy jabbing needles into people (just joking...about the nurse, not the injection).

Smoke Attack

We all know that smoking is nasty for your lungs. It can cause cancer and other diseases such as emphysema, which makes breathing difficult. Smoking also stains your teeth, nails and skin. It deadens your taste buds and your sense of smell as well.

One of the worst things that smoking does to your body involves the circulatory system. Carbon monoxide from cigarette smoke damages the inside of the blood vessels. Like sticking a caulking gun up your blood vessels, it hardens and clogs the veins and arteries so blood can't flow through properly. As a result, less oxygen is transported by the blood, and all the body's cells start to suffer. Poor circulation makes people who smoke two to three times more likely to have a clot block the supply of blood to the heart. When that happens, it's called a heart attack!

Veiny Veins

The first time I saw my grandmother's lower legs, I really stared at those blue, lumpy streaks that ran from the back of her knees to her ankles. I was just a kid, but it shocked me. I knew they were her veins, but I thought they were going to pop out of her skin. They must have caused her pain, because Grandma always complained about her achy, tired legs. No wonder! If I had them, I'd be afraid to walk, too!

My Grandma had varicose veins, from the Latin word "varix," which means "dilated vein." Sometimes you can see thin, blue lines through your skin. Those are veins, which carry blood to your heart. They go there to fill up with oxygen, like a car fills up with gas at a gas pump. Over time, the walls of the veins on your legs can get stretched and flabby. They can be painful and sometimes need to be removed (stripped) or injected.

Piles of Piles

When you get swollen veins on your anus (rear end), they're called hemorrhoids or, sometimes, piles. They can be terribly itchy and irritating. Hemorrhoids can be hereditary or caused by pregnancy or by simply straining on the toilet. Supposedly, Napoleon had them, which gives a whole new meaning to "Waterloo."

Red as a Beet

You're embarrassed. You're angry. You've just run a mile. You're caught outside in a snowstorm. You're sweltering because the air conditioning isn't working. Emotions, exercise, hot and cold temperatures—they can all make blood rush to the tiny capillaries near the surface of your skin. When this happens to us, it's called blushing, but the outcome is the same whatever the cause. Every square inch of your skin contains 20 feet of blood vessels. No wonder getting red-faced happens so fast!

Clot a Lot

Scrape your knee? Slice open a finger? Platelets are going to rush to the scene and call up the fibrins, or little threads that make a web to help plug the wound. This clotting makes the blood turn sticky and clumpy. Let the clot dry out for a while, and you've got a perfectly crusty scab! It'll stay there until new skin forms underneath and the scab falls off.

Scab Candy

You've probably seen those gross candies in specialty stores; you know, the ones that look like barf, poop or snot. There's even earwax candy. It's a plastic ear full of goopy, sugary sweet gel. All you have to do is take the accompanying plastic spoon and scoop out the earwax, er, candy gel, and yum, have fun.

Now, believe it or not, one candy company has come out with candy scabs. It's candy hidden inside a small plastic compartment under an adhesive bandage. When you get the urge to lick a scab, just go after your candy scab instead.

Colorful Bruises

Bump into this. Bang into that. Before you know it, you've got splotches of tender, darkened skin on your arms, legs, hips, wherever. Bruises, or contusions, can look icky—after all, doctors call them ecchymoses. Get it? Icky...ecchy?

Ecchymoses are injuries to the blood vessels just under your skin. Your skin doesn't break when you get a bruise, but underneath is a whole different story. The fragile blood vessels rupture and blood leaks out. Why are bruises so colorful? It's the clotting process. Here's what happens when we spin the wheel of color. First, the bruise looks red—fresh blood is seeping out of the vessels just under your skin. Next, a day or two later, hemoglobin makes the bruise turn dark purple, almost blue or black. After a few days, the bruise changes to a green or yellow color. One to two weeks later, it is light brown with a hint of yellow until it finally fades away.

If you do get a bruise, try to elevate the area and put something cold on it right away to slow down the blood flow.

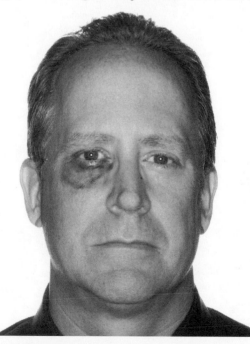

That might not stop the bruising completely, but it can help make the bruise less noticeable.

Reach for the Raw Steak
"Whoa! Nice shiner!"

It's hard not to notice a black eye. Dark blue, purple or black bruises around the eye stand out like a neon sign. Everyone wants to know how you got it. If a ball, door knob, elbow or anything smacks you in the eye or forehead, the delicate blood vessels just under the skin break. The soft tissue around your eye bruises easily, and the next thing you know, you've developed what doctors call ecchymosis—a black eye! It may look startling, but it usually isn't serious unless the eye itself is injured.

Boxers get black eyes all the time. Their trainers immediately put a very cold piece of metal over their eyes to help stop the bleeding and reduce swelling. Your mom may give you a raw steak, but a cold compress is probably better, and cheaper.

Dear Dr. Gross

Do I have both red and blue blood in my body? Why doesn't the blue blood ever come out?

Signed,
Bloody Confused

Dear Bloody:

Sorry, even if you are royalty, you don't have a drop of blue blood in you. Human beings have red blood (apparently Vulcans have green blood, but I've never seen one in my practice). Red blood cells contain hemoglobin, which has iron in it. Oxygen in the air we breathe clings to hemoglobin, and that oxygenated blood, such as the stuff that flows through your arteries or gets exposed to air through a cut, is a bright red. The blood within your veins contains very little oxygen and is actually very dark red. It only looks blue in the veins visible on your wrists or neck because of the way light is reflected through your skin.

Contrary to popular belief, members of the royal family don't have blue blood—their blood is the same red color as everyone else's. However, the blood in horseshoe crabs really is blue because it contains copper instead of iron and that gives it a bluish color.

Gushers

It sounds much more serious if you call it by its scientific name, a case of epistaxis. Nosebleeds are common. They can be caused by dry air, allergies, or even by picking your nose too much. High altitudes can break the delicate blood vessels inside your nasal cavity, too, and cause them to bleed. That's why they call the cheap seats way up on the upper levels of a concert hall or sports stadium the "nosebleed section"!

Spleen: The Blood Graveyard

Nothing lasts forever, not even the lowly blood cell. Each red blood cell only lives about 60 days. Those days are spent traveling around the circulatory system, transporting oxygen and taking away carbon dioxide.

Where do red blood cells go to die? Usually to an organ in the upper left of your abdomen called the spleen. It's one of those organs that stretches out several hours after you eat a big meal, then shrinks again. It's also where the worn-out red blood cells reach the end of the line. They get trapped and swallowed up by macrophages. But what about people who have had a splenectomy; that is, their spleen has been surgically removed? No problem. The liver and bone marrow contain macrophages, whose job it is to engulf old blood cells, so that's what they do.

Nuts 'n' Bolts of BONES

If you had x-ray eyes that could see right through flesh, everyone would look as though he or she were a walking skeleton. That's right, a shopping mall crowd would be something like a Halloween store come to life. It might seem strange, but underneath our skin and muscles are bones—all 206 of them, unless you're a newborn baby. In that case, you have 300 bones until a few here and there fuse together as you grow. As scary as skeletons might look in a Halloween store, without bones we'd be in shambles. Lose our bones, and we'd fall to the ground looking like a lumpy, limp pile of tissues.

Bones come in all shapes and sizes—long, flat, short, rounded and some just have weird shapes, period.

Think of bones as the framing on a house. Bones are actually a type of connective tissue and make great framing construction material. They're light and strong, but don't think each bone is the same as any old two-by-four from the lumberyard. On the contrary, bones are very much alive. Living bone is full of thousands of little canals for blood vessels and nerves. That's why if you break a bone, it hurts!

The human thigh bone, also called the femur, is the longest bone in the body and stronger than concrete. But unlike concrete, our bones can squeeze together a bit. Exercise keeps them strong, and if you don't use your bones at all, they become brittle. They tend to become thinner and more fragile in old age, so all the more reason to keep active.

Honing In on Bones

Not many of us really want to see our bones. Most of us don't have that opportunity unless we're witness to a compound fracture. That's a broken bone that pokes up through the muscles and skin, or a cut deep enough to reach bone. Ewww! But if you could see living bone (and get over the gross factor), you would see:

- an outer thin tissue layer full of blood vessels and nerves (called the periosteum)

- a hard part that contains canals and bone cells (the compact bone); it's strengthened by calcium, a mineral found in milk and certain green vegetables

- a spongy layer (the cancellous bone) that looks like a sponge; it's made of bony spikes that keep the bone light but strong

- a long tube in the middle that usually contains the jelly-like red or yellow marrow

I Have a Tail!

Yes, everyone does...well, sort of and not really. You might not even think twice about whether or not you have a tail until you fall on it, your tailbone, that is. At the end of your vertebral column (the bottom of your spine) are four or five small bones fused into one. That's your coccyx, or tailbone, and if you were an animal, it would probably support a tail.

Every once in a while, a baby is born with a growth that resembles a tail but doesn't contain any cartilage or bone. Apparently, the longest "tail" on record belonged to a 12-year-old boy and was more than six inches in length. Now, if you had one, would you want it removed? Think of how popular you would be at parties!

Bones that Float

There are bones in your body that float. Come again? They aren't attached to any other bones, so they are called "floating bones." Your kneecap (also called a patella) is one. It protects one of the biggest joints in the body, the knee joint.

You also have four floating ribs; they only hang by muscle and are not attached to the spine. If you count your ribs, you'll find seven pairs of **true** ribs at the top of your rib cage, and below them are three pairs of **false** ribs. The true ribs are called that because, unlike the false ones, they attach directly to the long, flat sternum or breastbone.

You should have 12 pairs of ribs, or 24 ribs, unless you are the one out of every 20 people who have either an extra pair or are missing a pair, or your name is Adam, and you're apparently the first man, and God took out one of your ribs while you were asleep!

Gnawing on a Bone

If you were a cannibal (a person who eats other people as meat) and wanted the biggest bone in the body to chew on, you should pick the ilium. It's the bone that makes up the hip, or pelvis. If you wanted to gnaw on the strongest bone, take the mandible or jaw bone. Don't even bother with the stapes, the tiniest bone. Even if you could find one where it's located deep in the middle ear, the stapes is only the size of this letter "U" and not worth the search—it doesn't have much meat on it.

Meet Ya at the Joint

Friend: "Hey, I'll meet you at that joint across the road."

You: "You mean the doughnut shop?"

Friend: "Yeah, that joint. We'll have some hot chocolate and doughnuts."

1st Bone: "Hey, I'll meet you at the joint."

2nd Bone: "You mean, the end of me?"

1st Bone: "Yeah, that joint. We'll have some synovial fluid."

That's right. Two bones meet at a joint. Some joints resemble hinges and move up and down, such as your jaw. Some, such as the wrist, also move forwards and backwards. Others, such as the sutures in your skull, don't move much at all. There are also ball-and-socket joints, such as the shoulder joint. These joints look the same as their names. And a dislocated bone is one that has (ouch!) slipped out of its joint.

Creaky Knees

Do your knees creak like an old door? Do they knock, knock, knock, even if nobody's home? You might have crepitus, that crunchy, crackly sound your joints make when you bend them. Popping pockets of air are called crepitus, too, so it can also be heard in the lungs.

There's a story that says Crepitus was the name of a Roman god—the god of farts. The story's probably untrue, since no one has proof that the Romans worshipped a god named Crepitus. But don't you think it would be a cool name for a Rottweiler or Doberman dog (especially one that farts a lot)?

Tending to Tendons

What about those icky-looking bands attached to muscles and bones? They are the ligaments and tendons. Ligaments are tough bands of fibrous tissue that attach one bone to another. Tendons attach muscle to bone. They're tough but don't stretch. The tendon at the back of each heel is called the Achilles tendon. In Greek mythology, Achilles' mother dipped him into the river Styx to make him immortal. She held him by the heel, so that became his only vulnerable spot.

Oh, My Aching Bones

Poor Quasimodo. His name meant "half-formed," but he simply had a terrible bone problem. It wasn't his fault, just like the millions of people whose bones aren't as straight as others. The reason could be congenital (meaning you're born with it) or because of some injury or disease.

Arthritis is a very common bone disease. It's been around for ages; even prehistoric people had it.

Some forms of arthritis weaken the tendons and ligaments around a joint until it becomes deformed. Arthritis can be bearable one moment or extremely painful at other times. You've probably heard people complain that their "arthritis is acting up," meaning that it feels like a pain in the bone!

Personal Shock Absorbers

When I was growing up, there was another part of our Sunday roast beef dinner that made my salivary glands work overtime. It was crunchy, chewy and uber-tasty all at the same time. We called it "gristle." It was really cooked cartilage.

In animals and people, cartilage is a strong and smooth fibrous tissue. It protects the bone ends in joints and acts like a shock absorber. Some of a baby's bones, such as the kneecaps, start off as cartilage and only turn to bone (or ossify) as the baby grows older. Cartilage can also be found in parts of your rib cage, nose and ears. Because cartilage doesn't have blood vessels, some people stick jewelry in it. Have you seen people who wear earrings that go way up the ear or through the nose? Now you know, those are cartilage piercings.

The Bump in Your Throat

Remember the story of Adam and Eve? Did you know that when Eve gave Adam the forbidden apple to eat, it got stuck in his throat? Well, that's the story behind the "Adam's apple." Everyone's got one, and it's not a piece of fruit bulging through your skin. It's actually hard cartilage protecting your larynx, or voice box. Men usually have a bigger Adam's apple than women, and that explains why teenage boys go through a crackly voice phase. Their Adam's apple is squishing their larynx. Oh joy.

Muscles and MEAT

Question: What do lions and most humans have in common?

Answer: Besides a love of steak, they both have approximately the same number of muscles—around 640!

There may be one other situation that could top the hypothetical Halloween store full of live skeletons—a store full of live skeletons covered in real muscles, and no skin! A scary sight, indeed, and one that's only a skin depth away. Muscles keep us going; without them we wouldn't be able to move. When they contract, or tighten, they pull on a bone, connective tissue or other muscle and tug us along to where we want to go. Muscles make up almost half of our body weight, unless you're an Arnold Schwarzenegger look-alike. Then it's probably more.

Meat My Muscles

Back to our Sunday roast beef analogy. Muscles are meat. When we slice through roast beef, we slice through animal muscle. When we bite the chunky dark meat off a chicken drumstick, we bite through leg muscle. If you look closely at your dinner meat, you'll see that it's made of fibers.

Muscle fibers. We've got the same sort of thing. Our muscles are our meat.

Muscles are made of fibers that get bigger with exercise. Each fiber (which is about as thick as a single hair strand) consists of a bunch of myofibers, which in turn consist of myofibrils. Each fibril has proteins (myosin/actin). Motor nerves send signals to muscle fibers and tell them what to do. There are striated, or striped, muscles (we control them), smooth muscles (such as intestines; we can't consciously move them) and heart muscles which is, of course, what your heart is made of. Cut a striped muscle in half and it might remind you of a cable full of wires. It has bundles of cords and filaments. Makes you want to become an electrician.

Muscle Prizes

The biggest muscle on the human body is the gluteus maximus—the buttock muscle. Yes, your butt wins the prize for your body's biggest muscle. And a tiny, thread-like muscle in your inner ear, the stapedius, wins for smallest muscle. And the busiest muscle? It's a shared prize, for the muscles in each eye. They contract about 100,000 times a day, even while you're sleeping!

Give It a Rest

Who hasn't complained of cramps? Cramps in your stomach, cramps in your leg, cramps in your fingers when you write too much. You can even get a cramp in your butt. When a muscle contracts and becomes tense and hard, it gives you a cramp. It's your muscles' way of saying, "Hey, we're working too hard. Give us a rest!"

If a muscle is strained or pulled, then you've probably torn some of the muscle fibers. If the tendons or ligaments tear, you've got a sprain. If you get a sprain in your lower leg, it's a great excuse to put your feet up on your desk.

Creepy Crackles

You can "crack" your knuckles because there is liquid in the space between your joints called synovial fluid. The synovial membrane covers the joints. Like oil lubricant for a car's engine, synovial fluid is thick and slippery enough to prevent wear and tear on the joints and keeps their movements smooth. When you crack your knuckles or tug on your phalanges (that's another word for your digits, or your fingers and thumb), you make a little vacuum where bubbles in the fluid can "pop." It's not harmful, but the sound can make other people cringe. Be polite and excuse yourself: "Sorry, my synovial fluid just imploded."

CHEESE!

Your face has about 50 muscles, and it takes 17 muscles to smile and 43 to frown.

Dear Dr. Gross

When Mom makes a turkey dinner, I always eat the white meat. My dad, however, loves the dark meat. I was wondering, if our muscles are our "meat," would people have white and dark meat, too?

Signed,
I Am Not A Cannibal

Dear Not A Cannibal:

The turkey's dark meat that your dad loves comes from red muscles usually found in the legs and thighs. Turkeys usually walk around a lot, and the muscle fibers in legs need the most oxygen to work harder and longer. The white meat, like the turkey breast, doesn't need as much oxygen because those muscles are used for short bursts of activity. You might see a domestic turkey fly a few feet but not as far as a duck or other bird. If you have ever eaten duck, you'll find that it is almost all dark meat.

I have never eaten a human, but I can tell you that most of our muscles are a mixture of white and dark meat. The muscles in our back and calves are mostly red muscle (or dark meat). As for white meat, that would come from the tiny muscles that make our eyes move and dart around quickly. Not much there for an all-white meat muscle nugget, though!

Human Pretzels

Know any people who say they are double-jointed? Do they wrap their legs up around their shoulders just to prove their human-pretzel capabilities? Well, boast as they might, you can tell them that they don't actually have any more joints than the rest of us. Sure they can get into weird positions, but that's just because they have super-stretched, long tissues called ligaments that connect bones together.

Puny Purses

Hundreds of tiny, fluid-filled sacs hang around in places where muscles and tendons contact bone. They're called bursae, from the Latin "bursa," which means "purse." The sacs even look like little purses, but you won't find any money in them, just fluid. This fluid minimizes friction and keeps the joints in working order. Bursae are quiet, hard workers that don't complain until they get sore or inflamed. When that happens, they get bursitis and probably feel as if they are going to burst!

The Not-So-Funny Bone

Newsflash: The "funny bone" isn't a bone at all. It's actually the ulnar nerve behind your elbow, and hitting or knocking it isn't funny, as I'm sure you've already found out. The feeling is better described as more of a tingly sensation. This happens when the ulnar nerve is banged against the long bone in your upper arm. The good news is that you can't break the funny bone! Now that's funny!

Bathroom GROSS

MEAL Adventures

What's your favorite meal? Mine is steak and kidney pie. I know, it's actually the striated muscle and organs of a cow, mixed with a gravy made from its blood and fat, all boiled to perfection. That may sound revolting to some people, but to me it's delicious.

Well, whatever your special lunch or dinner might be, imagine, if you will, the 30-foot-long journey your meal takes through your body. That journey is the digestive process and can take anywhere from 15 to 48 hours to complete. It starts even before you take your first forkful and ends in one of two places: your cells or the toilet.

Hungry Yet?

Before you even start your meal, your nose smells that yummy lunch and your eyes see it on the table in front of you. Those messages zoom to the brain, and that starts the ball rolling. The faucets of your salivary glands turn on full blast, and your stomach releases a hormone called gastrin. Your stomach starts to produce the digestive juices it will need when the food gets there.

Where is the food? You're shoving it into your mouth. And that's where digestion begins. Your incisors—those pointy eyeteeth—rip at that lunch, while your flatter molars macerate (soften) and chew it into a pulp. Enzymes in your saliva start to break down the food, and your tongue rolls it into a clumpy ball-shape, which is just the right size to go down the esophagus and into your stomach.

The Sickening STOMACH

Beneath your ribs, on the left side of your abdomen, sits your stomach. It's a J-shaped, muscular bag that works like a food processor, without the buttons to press. Instead, it has a slimy inside lining full of crevices, the gastric pits. This gastric lining spews out six to nine cups of digestive juices every day, including an enzyme called pepsin. That's "pepsi" (like the soft drink) with an "n." Pepsin isn't thirst quenching, but it's very good at breaking down food into simpler molecules.

Gastric juices also contain hydrochloric acid, which is so strong it zaps anything that touches it. Any bacteria, bits of snot, insects, flies or stray hairs that may have been on your food are destroyed in your stomach. Thank goodness.

Slimy Lining

OK, here's a question. If the stomach makes such strong acid (gastric juices), why doesn't the stomach eat itself out? The answer is that cells lining your stomach secrete a slimy mucus that protects the stomach. About half a million of these epithelial cells are shed every minute, and the whole lining is replaced every three days. Your stomach needs to keep producing a new layer of mucus, or yes, it would munch away on itself. So that mucus is important; it's a barrier and a lubricant. It's better than WD-40!

Gut Busters

How much can a stomach hold? A good five-course meal? In the 1890s, a German doctor wanted to find out how much a stomach could really hold. He filled the stomachs of dead bodies until they burst and concluded that the stomach could hold about one gallon.

There are exceptions, of course. Just ask anyone who enters one of those pie-eating competitions. Your stomach does stretch, but it doesn't shrink if you always eat smaller meals. There is an operation for people who are very overweight that actually reduces the stomach to the size of a golf ball. With such a small stomach, these patients eat smaller meals and find they lose weight quickly.

The Big Breakdown

Once food gets into your stomach, various enzymes get straight to work. Food is digested more easily because of certain enzymes. One such enzyme is lactase, which breaks down lactose. People who don't have enough lactase can have problems digesting products with lactose, such as milk. That's why you might see milk products labeled with "added lactase" on the grocery shelves. The manufacturer puts the lactase enzyme

WOW!

In a lifetime, the average person eats about as much as the weight of six elephants.

Dear Dr. Gross

Uh oh. My friend just told me that my stomach can't digest gum properly, and that it will sit in my stomach for seven years. Is this true? I've been swallowing my chewing gum since I was four years old...and now I'm 14!

Signed,
Gummy Tummy

Dear Gummy:

Don't worry. I can guarantee you there are no huge wads of gum sitting in your stomach. Chewing gum contains a gum base, which is why it has a rubbery texture. Like many things we eat, gum base contains ingredients our stomachs and intestines can't digest. The stuff that can't be absorbed by the body simply comes out the other end. Most of your chewing gum was converted into poop and flushed away long, long ago.

into the product so that people can enjoy it without the gas, bloating and tummy aches that they might otherwise experience.

Holey Moley!

In 1822, a Canadian voyageur named Alexis St. Martin was accidentally shot in the stomach. Remarkably, St. Martin survived and his wound healed, but it left a small hole through which his surgeon could actually observe stomach absorption. Bits of cotton-wrapped food were attached to a string, placed in the hole and later pulled out to see how much had been digested. The surgeon even tasted the partially digested food to test its acidity level. Yuck!

Chugging along the Chyme

Your stomach turns anything you have ingested into a thick, soupy substance called chyme. Depending on what you've ingested, chyme is often a creamy white or tan color. If you've eaten a lot of red Jell-O, strawberry ice cream and grape pop, the chyme might have more of a pinkish tinge.

Chyme usually continues on its journey through the alimentary canal to the duodenum. The duodenum is the beginning of the small intestine. Occasionally, the chyme doesn't makes it that far. If you have the flu, feel sick, stick a finger down your throat, or just flunked math, chyme might come back up through your mouth as vomitus (coming up in the next section).

I THINK I'M GONNA...

Puke. What's puke? It's vomit. What's vomit? It's simply chyme—chyme that made its way back up your esophagus and usually out of your mouth. You might know the act of vomiting (doctors called it emesis) by some of its other terms:

- barfing
- hurling
- ralphing
- spewing your guts
- talking to the big white telephone
- throwing up
- tossing your cookies
- upchucking

The longer the time between your last meal and when you puke, the smoother the vomit will be. That's because your stomach has been actively digesting your meal, and the big recognizable chunks (strings of spaghetti, bits of vegetables and so on) have already been broken down into that lovely liquidy chyme.

The Puke Process

If you have a friend very interested in the field of emetology, be warned. That's the study of nausea and vomiting. Nausea is that queasy tummy, sickly feeling in your throat and that dizziness you get before you puke. The word "nausea" comes from the Greek for "ship," as in "sick on a ship" or "seasickness."

Before you vomit, your salivary glands step up saliva production. That's because vomit is full of acid and can eat away at the enamel on your teeth. The more spit in your mouth, the more protection your teeth have from the powerful stomach/puke acids. You might also sweat, and your heart often beats a little faster.

The next thing that happens is an automatic reflex. You gag, and your stomach contents are automatically forced up your esophagus and out of your mouth. If you are not leaning over a toilet at this time, you've just puked all over the place. Why did all this happen? There are a lot of reasons:

- a virus, such as the flu
- an infection or inflammation in your stomach or digestive system
- food poisoning
- being in an accident or banging your head (concussion)
- motion sickness
- hormones (for example, morning sickness in pregnant women)

- certain drugs or alcohol
- being nervous
- seeing or smelling (or maybe even reading!) something gross

Once you actually do vomit, you usually feel better, unless the queasy, nauseous feeling comes around, again!

When Your World Spins

Throwing up in the backseat of a car. Reaching for the puke bag on an airplane. Leaning over the rails of a ship or riding on a roller coaster after eating a double cheeseburger. Everyone has a story about their motion sickness. More than half of all kids have puked in a car at one time or another.

A person who has motion sickness will keep feeling sick until the motion stops. The nauseous feeling is caused by the brain getting mixed messages. Your inner ear (which regulates balance) tells you one thing, but your eyes tell you another. The response is that the brain tells your body to throw up.

Virtual Vomiting

You can even get motion sickness from watching a movie that has a lot of action, or from playing video games, especially the 3-D kind. Gamers call this sensation "simulator sickness." It also happens in the flight simulators used by military trainers. If you start feeling dizzy at the controls, do yourself a favor and take a break—hopefully before the puke hits the console!

Spinning in Space

In space, there is no gravity. That's why you see astronauts on TV floating around their space shuttle like jellyfish in the sea. There is no up or down either, so the human brain can get very confused. One astronaut said that when he woke up in orbit, his arms and legs seemed to have vanished. When he consciously tried to move his arm, it suddenly reappeared!

BLECH!

Retching is wretched. It's also called the "dry heaves." That's when you go through the motions of vomiting, but nothing actually comes out. All the feeling but no puke.

The strange effects of zero gravity can make astronauts also feel dizzy and nauseous. It's called space sickness, and researching it is a top priority at space agencies such as NASA. In training, astronauts ride a KC-135 airplane that flies in arcs, which allows the riders to experience short periods of weightlessness. The plane has been nicknamed the "vomit comet," because first-time astronauts often get sick on it.

For Nausea, Press Here

Acupressure is an ancient remedy for many complaints. It involves gentle pressure on specific points of the body. The next time you feel nauseous, try this. Spread out one hand, palm down, and, with the other hand, put gentle pressure on the web between your thumb and index finger. Massage it for a few minutes. Feel better? You can also rub the top of your foot and in between the second and third toes. Ah, that feels good...

Intense INTESTINES

Imagine

a long, coiled-up snake right under your stomach. Those are your intestines. Your food, which turns soupy thick in the stomach, travels through them the way a rabbit would through a boa constrictor. Your intestines squeeze and push their contents along by wave-like muscle contractions called peristalsis. Eating helps this process, which is why most people have to use the bathroom after they eat!

The Small Sausages

The small intestine isn't so little—for the average adult it's about 21 feet long. Think of a long string of sausages all wound together. That's what the small intestine resembles.

Speaking of sausages, did you know that those pork and beef ones you see in the meat department were traditionally the stuffed small intestines of pigs and cows?

Back to human organs. Once food leaves the stomach as chyme, it squeezes through a valve called the pyloric sphincter. You know of another famous sphincter—your anus (or butt hole)—and both are tight muscle rings. The pyloric sphincter squirts chyme into the first section of the small intestine, the duodenum. There it mixes with bile from the liver and digestive juices from the pancreas. Over the next three to six hours, the small intestine absorbs as many goodies from the chyme as it can. To do this, it gets the villi working (see next section).

Forest of Fingers

The villi are like a velvety shag carpet of tiny fingers lining the small intestine's folded inner surface. Each villus is super tiny, and its job is to sweep up nutrients from digested food so they can be absorbed into the bloodstream. If you could spread out the absorption area of the small intestine, you'd have a flat, slimy section the size of a tennis court.

The Big Sausages

By the time food has passed through the small intestine, it's turned into a pasty, undigested sludge. It travels through another sphincter (the ileocaecal sphincter) and enters the colon, the largest part of the large intestine. Here, the water will get sucked out of it for the next 12 to 36 hours. Any leftover stuff gets chugged along and eventually goes down and then out.

Your colon is segmented, making it look like an accordion in a long, winding tube. The walls of the colon are muscular and move the sludge, now complete with paste-like poop (feces), much more slowly than the small intestine does. These movements can be mixing

WEIRD!
Your intestinal lining is almost twice as large as your skin area. The small intestine is about an inch wide, but the large intestine is two and half times that width.

and churning, like a squishy "poop blender," or peristaltic, which means shoved along as if the poop were in a giant wave pool. There can also be a mass movement, or one big push. This happens, too, in the last part of your colon, the rectum, when you "take a poo" (defecate).

The rectum is a thick, muscular layer, the last few inches of which is your "poop chute"—the anal canal. It has an internal and external sphincter. The first one you don't have any control over, but the second one you do (well, most of the time).

Letting it All Hang out

Torture is more than creepy under any circumstance, but one method of torture used for centuries was especially sickening. The victim's abdomen was slit open and his intestines slowly pulled out and wound around a barrel... while he watched!

That Worm-Like Thing

It doesn't do much. It simply hangs there. If it disappeared, you wouldn't even need it. What is it? It's your appendix, a tube located near the area where the small and large intestines meet. A fancy name for it is the vermiform appendix, which comes from the Latin for "worm-like." Don't feel bad if doctors have to take yours out if it gets infected (that's appendicitis). After all, who wants a worm-like thing in their abdomen, anyway?

Pee, Poops and TooTS

PEE PEE foR BEGINNERS

Every minute, your kidneys act like coffee machine filters. They take in about five cups of blood and cleanse it. But instead of dripping water through a filter to make coffee, blood filters through the kidneys and comes out as a waste liquid. The waste and extra water is urine, a yellow liquid also known as pee.

Pee is mostly water, along with ammonia (which the liver turns into urea), some salts and other waste products.

The pee collects in a funnel (called the renal pelvis), then is pushed along two long tubes (called ureters) to the bladder. Your bladder is one stretchy organ, so if you're sitting in a movie theater and don't want to miss a second of the action, your bladder will just keep storing the urine until the credits role and you finally go to the bathroom.

Urine can come out looking either bright or pale yellow, even orangey or cloudy, depending on what you've eaten. When you don't drink enough fluids, it can look darker, because it's more concentrated. As you probably know, the more you drink, the more you excrete. If you downed a few of those giant gulp drinks during that movie, you're going to be peeing for a very long time. If you sweat, you'll pee less, because you are losing water in your body through perspiration. Although sweat is salty, it's (thankfully) not the golden color of pee. If that were the case, we'd all be very grossed out indeed.

I Have to Go Again

We have an advantage here on solid Earth. The pee in our bodies tends to trickle downwards. In space, however, there is no gravity. If you are floating around in zero gravity, your brain gets confused because some of the pee "goes up" and makes your bladder feel full. Your brain keeps getting the message that you need to go pee, even if you REALLY don't have to.

The History of Pee

Throughout history, urine has been one of the most useful liquids people make. It contains urea and uric acid, which makes urine a convenient wound cleanser. By tasting or smelling it, people could often tell what type of illness someone had. Some cultures even recommended drinking healthy urine as a cure for ailments.

Dear Dr. Gross

Why does my pee stink after I eat asparagus?

Signed,
Reluctant To Eat Asparagus

Dear Reluctant:

If you can smell stinky pee after eating asparagus, be happy! Believe it or not, some people can't. It has to do with chemicals in the asparagus that are broken down in the urine. Asparagus contains asparagusic acid (younger, white asparagus seems to have more of this acid). Your body breaks this acid down into a sulfur compound that includes a stinky chemical called mercaptan. Scientists think that either certain people don't produce the gene to break down the amino acids in digested asparagus or that their sensory cells can't pick up the sulfur compounds in the asparagus. Either way, don't let the funny pee smell stop you from eating asparagus. It's a healthy vegetable loaded with vitamins, minerals, folic acid and fiber. So hold your nose and chow down. Bon appetit!

Fresh urine has been used in tanning hides and dyeing clothing. It's great for removing oils and dirt. During the Middle Ages, servants were hired to stamp on wool in large vats of urine. The urine drew the greasy lanolin out of the wool so it could be spun into super soft cloth. Does that mean that the most fashionable medieval color was... pale yellow?

The Color of Pee and Poo

There is a question that has stumped humankind since the dawn of civilization. It's up there with "What is the meaning of life?" The burning question (and hopefully it isn't too burning) is this: Why is pee yellow and poop brown?

The answer comes from the largest organ inside your body, the liver. In an adult, it's as big as a football and does everything from storing energy, processing nutrients and taking poisons out of your blood to making a substance called bile. Bile contains an orange-brown pigment called bilirubin, which comes from dead, decomposing red blood cells. Bilirubin can be broken down even further to urobilins, which give pee that yellowy color. Urobilin gets more concentrated in the intestines and mixes with the solid waste (feces), giving it a nice brown color.

WOW!

The average bladder holds about two cups of urine.

Of course, you've probably noticed that pee and poop can vary in their shades. The poop of young babies is called meconium and is more yellow than brown. That's because infants' intestines don't have all the bacteria found in adult intestines. If you are sick, ingest a lot of food coloring or eat tons of green leafy vegetables, your poop might turn out yellow, black or green!

HMMM...

No country has the color brown in the background of their national flag... I wonder why....

Other words for "poop" are "feces" and "stool." "Stool" comes from the old word "stol," which meant the seat someone sits on to go poop. "Feces" is from the Latin "faex," which means "dregs," or the part that nobody wants.

THE LOWDOWN ON POOP

You know it as doo doo, caca, log or turd. Some people call it feces, excrement or a "BM" (bowel movement). To have one is to do number two, take a dump, drop a load, pinch a loaf, evacuate your bowels or, as scientists say, defecate.

Yes, poop is what comes out of you after everything you've eaten has been digested. It consists mostly of water, along with bacteria, fats and indigestible stuff, which is why you might occasionally find a seed or kernel of corn in the, um, toilet.

Your poop actually can tell a great deal about what you eat. High-fiber foods, such as fruits, vegetables and whole grains, make your poop bigger and looser. If you always eat more animal-based foods, such as meats and dairy products, you might notice that your poop is smaller and heavier.

When it comes to poop size, how big is "big"? That depends. A really huge poop can weigh as much as half a pound! And interestingly, kids have bigger poop for their body weight than adults.

And if you are wondering why some poop stinks and others don't, again, it depends on what you have eaten. The billions of bacteria in your intestines break down undigested waste molecules into certain compounds, some of which are super smelly, indeed. That's when an open window or a can of air freshener come in handy!

Word of the Day
(Impress your teacher with this one.)

Scybalum (pronounced scy'-bal-am; plural is scybala): A dry, hard lump of poop; it can resemble a frozen chocolate bar.

Which Poo Do You Do?

When you see your poop in the toilet, what's the first thing that comes to your mind? Right! A description! In other words, "It looks like..." and you fill in the blank. In 1997, the Bristol Stool Chart was developed in England to help doctors identify different poop shapes. According to this scale, stool can be in one of seven forms:

Type 1: Separate, hard lumps, similar to nuts

Type 2: Sausage-shaped and lumpy

Type 3: Sausage-like but with cracks on surface

Type 4: Sausage- or snake-like, smooth and soft

Type 5: Soft blobs with clear-cut edges

Type 6: Fluffy pieces with ragged edges; mushy

Type 7: Watery, no solid pieces, entirely liquid

Ugh. . . I've Got to Run

Diarrhea, it's brown and runny. Diarrhea, it's not funny.

It's especially not funny if you're the one who has it. You make mad dashes to the bathroom and back again. No wonder it's often called "the squirts." It comes out watery, like melted chocolate ice cream, and paints the toilet bowl various shades of fudge.

Diarrhea is loose stool. It occurs when your colon isn't absorbing as much fluid as it should. Too much diarrhea can make you dehydrated; that is, your body loses water. For babies and young children, diarrhea can be life-threatening.

So why does it happen? You may have irritated your bowels from eating oily or fatty foods, or you might have an underlying problem with your colon. People with serious diseases, such as dysentery or radiation sickness, usually have diarrhea as a symptom. Or you could simply be nervous. Students about to write a difficult exam often excuse themselves so that they can run to the toilet.

Most of the time, diarrhea is the body's way of getting rid of a bacterial or viral infection. Contractions in your bowels force all the fluid and contents out. You might have the flu, or maybe you ate something with salmonella bacteria—that's food poisoning, and you're probably puking at the same time.

Some people have irritable bowel syndrome. They get bad cramps and can have diarrhea or constipation and must be careful about what they eat. When kids get diarrhea, mothers often make them follow a BRAT diet (bananas, rice, applesauce and toast), because those foods are easily digested and can help alleviate diarrhea.

Montezuma's Revenge

"How was your trip, Johnny?" the teacher asks. "Didn't you get back last week? You must have loved the sun and beach. Did you get to practice your Spanish?"

Johnny manages a weak smile. "I was sick the day after I got there. I spent my whole vacation in the hotel room. I was still sick last week, that's why I wasn't at school."

"Oh, Montezuma's Revenge," says the teacher. "Happens all the time."

Several hundred years ago, a European explorer named Hernando Cortez arrived in Mexico. At first, everything was nice and cordial with the native chief, Montezuma. Then problems started and, to make a long story short, Montezuma placed a curse on future visitors. Montezuma's revenge. Doctors call it traveler's diarrhea. No matter what you call it, it's not a souvenir you want to bring home.

All Plugged Up

Try as you might, sometimes you just can't "go." Frequency varies, but most people have a bowel movement (they go poo) anywhere from one to three times a day to once every few days.

Constipation happens when all the water has been squeezed out of the stool, and it can't travel down the colon and rectum easily. It gets stuck. You're stopped up like a corked bottle. Do not pass Go. Do not collect $200.

Long ago, maybe when our ancestors were cave people, we'd just plop and go as we please. A shrub here, a bush over there; the world was one big toilet. Nowadays, we have to sit in class. We have to ride in buses and cars. We have to shop, meet a friend or watch the end of that movie. It's not always convenient to find a bathroom, so we hold it in. Our colons keep sucking the water out of the feces, and when we actually get around to sitting on the toilet, nothing comes out. The average North American diet of refined, processed and fast foods doesn't help either. We need fiber from fruits, vegetables and whole grains to keep the plumbing working properly.

As the saying goes, if you gotta go, you gotta go. Drinking water, exercising and eating healthy foods keep constipation away. Some people take stool softeners and laxatives to help "get the poo out."

What's an Enema?

You've heard the word. But what does it mean? An "enema" is shoving water or some other liquid up your rectum (your butt). Squirting the water up farther into the colon is called irrigation.

Enemas were popular in the 1920s, when people did them to clean out their insides. In reality, our intestines are fine with doing the housekeeping all by themselves. Today, enemas are usually given to patients before intestinal surgery or to relieve constipation.

Gross in the News

Do commercials for products that treat intestinal and anal ailments make you feel sick? Apparently they turn the stomachs of morning commuters in Beijing, China. After numerous complaints about these types of TV ads, which are shown on public transport, the city banned the offensive ads between the hours of 7 AM and 9 AM. Now go enjoy your breakfast!

Chowing Down

Ever seen a dog eat its own poop? The owner usually tugs on the dog's collar and shouts, "No, Fido, that's gross!" It may seem gross to us, but there are many animals that eat stool. It's called coprophagy, or ingesting feces. Researchers even found that rats who are prevented from eating their stool actually suffer from malnutrition.

Why we humans don't eat poo might be evolutionary. There's a lot of bacteria in feces, and our ancestors may have learned that eating it can pass on infections and make you very sick, or at least, disgusting. That's why we don't eat one another's vomit, too. It is interesting to note, however, that not all of the proteins and nutrients we ingest are absorbed by the body. That means that they come out in our stool, so stool can be nutritious (minus all the germs). However, the thought of eating poo is pretty well disgusting around the world. So, no worries about finding frozen poo burgers on the grocery shelf anytime soon, that's for sure.

Dear Dr. Gross

I had to write a test in class the other day. I could barely concentrate because my stomach kept making these strange sounds. Everyone laughed so hard. I know it wasn't the hungry stomach gurgles because I had just had lunch. Then again, I had eaten a double-layered burrito with spicy taco sauce. What were those weird noises?

Signed,
Loud Tummy

Dear Loud:

Those sounds are called borborygmi. It's a growling or grumbling in your stomach and intestines. Borborygmi comes from the Greek, meaning "to rumble." Gas and fluids are always pushed around by muscular contractions. Most people are familiar with those rumbling "hungry tummy" sounds, but borborygmi can occur just before you have diarrhea and can sound like a creature moaning and trying to escape from your guts.

The sounds that resemble long, loud farts can be among the most embarrassing! Often borborygmi are caused by having too much gas in your intestines or eating foods that you haven't completely digested. I'd bet the burrito did a number on your digestive juices.

BLOWING GAS: THE FART

If you fart in a bathtub, you get bubbles. And that's exactly what farts are—bubbles of gas coming out of your butt. Flatulence is the gas in us. If you have a gastrointestinal tract, you will produce flatulence—and some of us do that more than others.

When the gas actually comes out, it's called flatus, also known as a fart. The word "flatus" comes from Latin and means "to blow gas." Everybody farts. Even the Queen of England (I don't personally recall anyone who has actually said they heard her do it—but if you have, I'm dying to know the details!). When we fart, we've passed gas, broken wind, let one rip or cut the cheese! And that is exactly what most people do about 14 times a day, but, like the Queen, they usually don't admit it.

The In's and outs of Farts

What's in a fart? Gases such as oxygen, nitrogen, carbon dioxide, hydrogen and sometimes methane. How do those gases get in us? Farts are made from swallowed air or chemical reactions in our guts. They are also produced by the oodles of bacteria that live in our intestines.

The "swallowed air" type of fart usually doesn't smell too bad. When you eat, talk, or do anything that involves opening your mouth, you can't help but bring air into your stomach. Those gases are often nitrogen, carbon dioxide and oxygen. Oxygen usually gets absorbed by the body, but the other two gases sometimes squeak out the other end.

Farts are also made in the intestines by bacteria. As our food is digested, it travels down to the large intestine where over 400 different kinds of bacteria start munching away. As they eat the dead cells and whatever is leftover from the digested food, they poo out gases...and often very stinky ones at that! In the large intestine, when the gases mix with hydrogen sulfide (rotten egg smell) and ammonia (pee pee smell), they really stink. Those are the really hot, stinky farts and the silent but deadly or loud, smelly ones. If they happen to you, just blame it on the dog!

EWWW!

If you try to hold in a fart, it won't harm you. It'll simply back up, to return later. It might even come out in your sleep. Emperor Claudius, who ruled the Roman Empire from 41 to 54 AD, proposed a law that would allow people to fart at banquets. He didn't want his guests to worry about harming their health.

Floating farts

When you think about it, you should be able to see a fart. Breathing out through your mouth in very cold weather makes your breath look like a hazy, misty cloud. If your fart were concentrated enough, you'd think you should be able to see it, too. Underwear and pants might get in the way, but a fart is, after all, warm air exiting your body. You might not want to walk through it, though.

Like bad breath, farts contain certain molecules that give them their distinct smell. They are microscopic, but the fart has tiny "poop" molecules in it that can dissolve into the air or, if they are heavier, get left on solid surfaces. That's why if you fart while sitting in a chair, someone else can still smell it after you leave!

The fart of All farts

If a fart contains hydrogen or methane (both flammable gases), it can burn. Bacteria can produce methane, but most people don't have farts with methane. The one-third of the population that does, could see a "blue flame" if that fart were lit with a match, but lighting up your farts isn't recommended. It's very dangerous, and the last thing you want is a burned butt!

fossilized farts

Fossilized termites with their own fossilized farts have been found in amber. It is thought that microbes in the live termites—which were caught in sap—escaped and formed little bubbles next to the insects that were, in turn, fossilized. Interestingly, termites are also known for having digestive systems that fart out huge amounts for their size.

Whoever Smelt It, Dealt It

Maybe. Often, the farter is last to smell the fart because the odor is traveling away from him (unless he turns and walks into it, that is). The stink in a fart comes from chemical compounds called mercaptans. They are produced when bacteria in your intestines break down foods. Sulfides and mercaptans contain a chemical called sulfur, and some foods, such as meats and eggs, contain a lot of sulfur. If you eat large amounts of these foods, your farts will probably be extra smelly!

A Gassy Experiment

In 1998, two physicians from Minneapolis did an experiment to find out which chemicals made farts stinky. They took 16 healthy people and gave them beans for breakfast and dinner. The scientists then put a tube up each person's butt. When the subject passed gas (farted), the gas went down the tube and into a special bag. It was then collected in a syringe and put through gas chromatographic-mass spectroscopic analysis; in other words, a machine that could detect which specific gases were in the flatus (farts). They also had judges smell each syringe to determine how bad each fart smelled.

What did the experiment discover? The scientists found out that the average fart smell came from concentrations of hydrogen sulfide, methane thiol and dimethyl sulfide. They also found that women's farts had higher concentrations of dimethyl sulfide and actually smelled "stinkier." Men's farts tended to have a higher volume of gas, so in reality the smell worked out to about the same.

Letting one Rip

I'm sure you've played with balloons, blowing up but not tying them, then letting them zip around the room. You've probably also played with your anal sphincter, either shooting out a noisy fart or trying to squelch it. The balloon neck and your anal sphincter (the muscle in your anus) work much the same. It's the vibrations from both and how fast the air escapes from them that make a certain fart (or balloon) sound.

A tight sphincter has a small opening, resulting in a high-pitched, whiny fart. Looser sphincters have wider openings and make more of a "rumble" sound. Depending on the sound of your fart, you can always cover it up by saying you have creaky floors or a squeaky chair.

Fart Foods

The following foods frequently form foul farts:

- beans
- broccoli
- brussels sprouts
- cabbage
- cauliflower
- eggs
- milk
- most meats
- all-you-can-eat buffets...enjoy!

Josef Pujol: The "Fartiste"

Joseph Pujol was born in France in 1857. When he was a young boy, he went swimming one day and discovered that he could take up water into his rectum then squirt it out like a water gun. As an adult, Pujol tried this with air and found he could create fascinating fart sounds. The pitches and tones ranged from high and squeaky to ones as loud as a cannon or as long as 10-second rips.

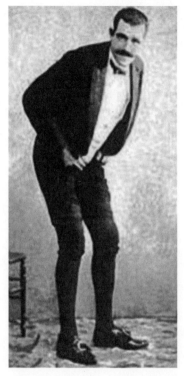

Pujol soon learned to make sounds identical to farm animals or musical instruments. By 1892, he was performing as "Le Petomane" (The Farter) in Paris' famous Moulin Rouge club. Spectators came from miles around to see the famous Pujol. He even performed for the King of Belgium. Pujol's success helped him support his wife and children. After World War I, Pujol retired from his show-biz life and settled down to manage a biscuit factory.

Farts in the News

Do your stinky farts embarrass you in public? Are you afraid to travel in airplanes or sit in meetings because a "smelly one" might escape? Your worries are over. An American underwear company has invented a pair of undies called "Under-Ease." Made of airtight fabric and sealed with elastic around the waistband and legs, the underwear will keep your farts contained, and a built-in, replaceable air filter will trap any foul odors. The inventor calls this underwear "protection against bad human gas."

farts that Are way out There

If you are in zero gravity, such as on a space shuttle, what happens to all those gases your body produces? Apparently, they can't exit your mouth as easily as they do on Earth. So, instead, they come out as farts. In other words, astronauts can be rip-roaring farting machines. Then again, if an astronaut could exit the capsule without a protective suit and fart in outer space, he or she would be propelled forwards—a mini fart rocket!

Disgusting
Dead Stuff
on your
BODY

The SKIN You're In

Skin.

It's the body's largest organ. If you peeled it all off, it would weigh as much as a big Thanksgiving turkey.

Skin. Like plastic wrap over a sandwich, it's a barrier against germs and keeps everything underneath from drying or falling out. Like an umbrella, it's a waterproof covering that shields us from the sun's burning rays. And we take it with us wherever we decide to wander!

Our skin is like a blanket—it's soft yet strong, flexible yet tough, and it keeps our body at just the right temperature. Doesn't skin sound all soft and cuddly? OK, as long as you realize that the very surface of the skin consists of dead cells. Yes, it's called the horny layer (or stratus corneum) and is full of dead skin cells, called keratinocytes. These keratinocytes contain keratin, which is the tough protein that makes up our skin, hair and nails.

The dead keratinocytes on our skin's surface are flattened and piled on top of each other like exercise mats in a gymnasium storage room. And they don't just sit there, they are constantly being shed. That's right, shed, as in rubbed or flaked off—gone, vamoose, no longer needed. It's similar to what a snake does when shedding its skin, except that's a much more interesting process and the snake gets a cool-looking "snake casing" afterwards. You shed 50,000 skin flakes every minute, about 50 million a day, but you hardly notice. By the time you are 70 years old, you will have lost over 100 pounds of skin cells!

Movin' on Up

So how did the skin cells get to the surface? That horny, dead layer of cells is at the very top of a thin, outer layer of skin called the epidermis. It doesn't have any blood vessels but has its own layers. The epidermis is super thin on your eyelids and extra thick on other areas, such as the soles of your feet.

Just below the horny layer are the living keratinocytes (also called squamous cells). They take about three or four weeks to shimmy up from a second, thicker layer of the skin, the dermis. Along with blood vessels, lymph vessels, hair follicles, nerves, sweat glands and other cells, the dermis contains proteins called collagen and elastin, which hold it together.

Under the dermis is the subcutaneous layer, which acts as a shock absorber for the skin. It contains fat cells as well as collagen. If you get an injury that goes down to this layer, well, that's one nasty cut indeed, and you'll probably end up with a deep scar.

Hard as a Rock

Have you ever heard someone described as "callous"? It's not a compliment; it means the person is insensitive. Your skin does something similar when you keep applying pressure on one spot—it forms a callus, and the area becomes less sensitive. Extra layers of dead skin build up to protect the softer tissue underneath. It's as though your skin is saying, "Hey, if you're going to pound me there, I'm getting a thicker skin!"

Calluses are common on the feet, hands, fingers—any place where there's constant pressure. When calluses develop a hard center, they are known as a "corn," perhaps because it feels as if a kernel is stuck on your skin or between your toes. Ouch!

Come to the Staph Party

Staph bacteria are happy (their real name is staphylococcus aureus, but they prefer the nickname "staph"), because there's an infection brewing in the armpit hair follicle. Party time! A boil party! The infection starts as a bump and gets bigger, redder and more swollen. The boil starts to heat up until in rush those white blood cells.

The next thing you know, the area is full of fluid. Not any old fluid, but that yellowish white stuff called pus that we talked about a while back. And just when that ugly inflammation gets as hot as a furnace...POP! The party's been busted. The boil, also called a furuncle, explodes, though sometimes it just subsides on its own. Either way, the pus drains away. Party's over. Until next time, that is.

Mr. Carbuncle

It sounds like someone's name. "Hi, my name is Carbuncle. I admit it, I'm a cluster of boils." And that's exactly what carbuncles are, one big skin abscess caused by a bunched up group of boils. If you look carefully, you might even see their "heads," little creamy-colored, pinprick spots filled with that lovely liquid—pus. Carbuncles look much worse than a solitary boil and so naturally take longer to heal.

Wrinkles and CRINKLES

Check out those skin cream advertisements in magazines and on TV. Do they mention collagen? It's an important protein that gives our skin its elasticity and strength and is also found in our tendons and ligaments. As we get older, collagen breaks down, and our skin can sag. We get little lines that grow deeper over the years and turn into wrinkles.

Slathering collagen-enriched cream on our skin doesn't replace the protein, but it does make our skin feel soft and smooth. There is even a rare skin disorder that causes collagen to become defective

Dear Dr. Gross

Why does my grandmother have wrinkles like an elephant? I only get them on my fingertips when I spend too long in the bath.

Signed,
Curious as a Mouse

Dear Curious:

Once upon a time, before she was born, your grandmother floated around inside the fluid-filled womb of your great-grandmother. Her baby skin was covered in waxy stuff called vernix, which stopped water from getting sucked out of it and making it wrinkle. If you've been swimming or soaking in the tub for quite a while, water leaves your skin and you start to wrinkle. But that's not what causes the wrinkles on your grandmother today. No, she got those from years and years of living.

Skin starts off smooth and soft because there is lots of fat under it (subcutaneous fat), but that layer gets thinner as we get older. Skin gets stretchier, too, and doesn't bounce back as easily. That's because connective tissues that hold the dermis and epidermis together aren't doing such a great job anymore. Frowning, smiling and squinting over and over again deepen the creases in the skin. Only surgery, such as a facelift, can get rid of these lines, but then again, aren't grandmothers supposed to have wrinkles?

and creates loose skin. People with this disorder have super stretchy skin.

oñ Your Mark ... Stretch!

If you dare, ask your mother if she has stretch marks. She'll probably show you the silvery thin lines on her abdomen and say, "Look what happened to my skin when I was pregnant with you!"

So what did happen? Well, as you got bigger inside your mother, her skin had to stretch quickly. The collagen in her dermis broke down and couldn't repair itself rapidly enough. So your mother was left with red, pink or purple scars that lightened over the years. Very large people who lose weight often get stretch marks, too.

Not-So Light Cellulite

Dimples are cute on babies, not so cute on thighs and butts. When lumpy bunches of fat collect under your skin and give it a puckered, orange-peel look, it's called cellulite. Some beauty salons claim to have creams and massages that can get rid of cellulite. They might temporarily make the skin look firmer, but that's about it. The only real way to eliminate cellulite is to lose body fat. Eat less, exercise more.

Very overweight people sometimes go to a doctor to have liposuction. That procedure sucks the fat out of places such as your thighs and abdomen, but it's usually the deeper fat that is removed. Because cellulite is close to the skin's surface, the person might appear thinner, but will still have the dimples!

The MOLE Story

Madonna had one, and later got it removed. Supermodel Cindy Crawford has a famous one on her upper lip. Odds are you know somebody who has a nevus. They are also known as moles, but they don't scurry blindly underground like the rodent kind. Moles can appear on any part of your body. They can be pink, light or dark brown, even blue or black. Most are round, but they can be any shape. Some are raised. Some are flat and appear in groups. It's as though a little constellation of moles twinkles on the surface of your skin.

One in 100 people are born with a mole, and moles usually appear before a person is fully grown. Hormonal changes, such as pregnancy, can make new moles show up here and there. You might notice moles popping up on your skin when you go through puberty. Moles run in families, so if your parents have tons of moles, you'll probably have a bunch of them, too.

Being out in the sun can cause moles to appear and to darken, and the same goes for freckles. Once in a while, a mole might develop skin cancer, but most moles are completely harmless. They seem to have a life of their own, though— a life that usually lasts a good 50 years. They can start out small, or not turn up for decades. They can get lighter or bigger, and some moles even sprout a hair or two.

If you have a big, hairy mole stuck in the middle of your face, you may decide to have it removed. A doctor can do this surgically or with a laser. That usually makes the mole sufferer much happier, except in rare instances when the mole actually grows back. In that case, you might as well keep your friendly mole. It probably missed you.

Melanie and the Melanocytes

I once knew a girl with freckles. They were like hundreds of tiny, brown speckles on her nose and her upper cheeks. There seemed to be more of them in the summer than winter, but this girl, let's call her Melanie, hated them all year round. She tried everything to get rid of them. She scrubbed her face with soap and water. That just made her skin dry. She heard that lemon juice might make them fade. It didn't work and only stung her eyes.

Melanie kept wishing her freckles would disappear, until she met a boy who thought they were cute. From then on, she didn't mind her freckles anymore. Then, one day, Melanie had an argument with her boyfriend. She was so upset, she ate 10 bags of carrots. The next morning, when she looked in the mirror, she saw that her skin had turned yellow. That was the day Melanie learned what the word "melanin" meant.

Everyone's skin contains cells called melanocytes. They produce a brown pigment called melanin, which gives skin, hair, even moles, their color. The darker someone's skin, the more melanin their melanocytes make in all their skin layers. Freckles are super-concentrated little dots of melanin.

Melanin shields skin layers from the sun's harmful ultra violet (UV) rays. Sun exposure, and using tanning salons, make melanocytes work overtime to produce more and more melanin. That's how people tan, unless they're among those fair-skinned groups with melanocytes that can't keep up. In that case, the UV rays fry the skin and, lo and behold, you have a painful sunburn!

As for the carrots Melanie ate, their orangey color comes from the high amount of a chemical they contain called carotene. Mix carotene and melanin and you get the yellow tint Melanie saw on her skin, which fortunately for her, was only temporary!

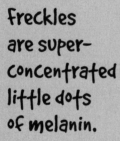

freckles are super-concentrated little dots of melanin.

Sweating BULLETS

Quick, count the number of holes on your face. Let's see, there's one mouth, two nostrils...oh, and about 20,000 little holes all over your facial skin. Relax, those are your pores and, unlike your mouth, they never close. Most pores are so teeny tiny you can't see them unless you peer very, very closely. Some people do have large pores. No matter what the size though, each pore is there for a reason. One of those reasons is to let the sweat out!

Gushing Glands

Our skin consists of three million little coiled tubes that go through the dermis and epidermis to the outside surface. They are the ducts for our sweat glands that secrete the watery, salty sweat. If you put each one end to end, you'd have almost 30 miles of sweat glands. We produce about 1.5 cups of sweat every day. A person running in hot weather could even lose enough sweat to fill up a large, plastic soda pop bottle. Care to take a swig?

Sniff, Sniff ... Get the Hint?

Most of your sweat comes from the eccrine sweat glands, which are found on your palms, armpits, forehead and soles of your feet. There is another type of sweat gland, the apocrine glands, that makes a thicker sweat. These glands get really active around puberty. That's when some older kids start realizing they might need to use deodorant.

The apocrine glands are also scent glands. Animals aren't the only ones who send messages through their odor—people do as well! You might not even be aware that you're giving off a specific scent. It has to do with pheromones in the fluid produced by the scent glands. Pheromones are chemicals that send a message. Animals and insects have all kinds of pheromones: the "keep away" one, or "this way to food" and the "beware" ones. They also produce pheromones for attracting mates, or in the case of humans, trying to get a date. Besides members of the opposite sex, the sweat from apocrine glands attracts something else—bacteria!

A Sticky Situation

If you think sweat itself is stinky, think again. Sweat itself is odorless. So why do we smell sweat? Once again, the answer is bacteria. You can't see them, but there are millions of them on every fingernail-sized piece of your skin.

Some of these bacteria love to munch away on the secretions from the apocrine sweat glands. An adult has about 2000 of these glands. Most are found in the armpits, groin and scalp. After the bacteria eat, they poop out chemical compounds as waste. It's this chemical poop on our skin that we smell.

Sweating It out

People have been sweating it out for centuries. Some cultures, many of them Eastern, have always placed a high priority on personal hygiene. In ancient times, bathing was often a social event. The Roman public baths were popular, and people met there sort of the way we meet at a coffee shop today. By the Middle Ages, plagues and other nasty epidemics made public bathing a risky activity. No one wanted to share their bathwater with a person covered in oozing blisters.

When people washed themselves, they did so "in parts." They took a bucket and sponge, washed one arm, then the other one and so on. Only the rich had the luxury of baths. Even then, daily baths were uncommon. You were lucky if you had a few baths a year. If you traveled and were stuck on a ship for months, the bacteria growth on your skin probably made you smell particularly foul. When the Japanese first met European explorers (who didn't bathe much) in the 17th century, they called them "bata-kusai," which means "stinks of butter."

Bye-Bye Bo

What do you buy the person who has everything, including stinky "BO" (body odor)? Fret no more. Now there's a new electronic device on the market that can help your foul-smelling friend. Tiny electrical currents zap your pores and plug up your sweat ducts. The sweat gland faucet is temporarily turned off, and you're free of BO and embarrassing underarm stains. The effect can last up to six weeks. Think of how much you can save on the cost of anti-perspirants!

The Great Bo Debate

Next time you are in a pharmacy, take a walk down the deodorant aisle. See the zillions of different brands of products for BO? There are sprays, roll-ons, gels or solids—you name it, someone has marketed it. Look closely and you'll see either "antiperspirant" or "deodorant" on the label. There's a reason for that. Antiperspirants plug up the glands and slow down sweat production. They contain wax, fragrance and an active ingredient that usually contains some type of aluminum compound. The aluminum makes cells in the ducts swell and close. The sweat can't get out. Deodorants, in contrast, just mask or kill the bacteria.

Which is better? People usually prefer one or the other, depending on how much they stink and how well their brand works. Others think it's unnatural to plug up the sweat glands.

Is It Hot in Here?

Imagine sweating all the time and you can't stop it. Perspiration pours down your face. Your hands are never dry, and your shirt is always drenched. Hyperhidrosis is a condition some people inherit. Regular antiperspirants don't work for them, but Botox injections do. Yes, that's the same treatment that rich, wrinkly women seek out for firmer, younger-looking skin. Botox temporarily paralyzes the tiny muscles in your face so you can't frown. It also stops sweat glands from working, and injecting it into the armpits prevents you from sweating so much.

Motor oil for the SKIN

Sebum

—a strange name for the oil produced by your skin—but it's from the Latin word meaning "fat." Sebum contains glycerides, fatty acids, waxy substances and cholesterol. Those sound as if they are junk food ingredients, but trust me, you don't want to eat them. Sebum is made in the sebaceous glands, which are all over the body except the palms of your hands and the soles of your feet. Special cells in these glands produce sebum until they burst open. The sebum then flows out like a little oily river.

Most of these sebaceous glands are attached to hair follicles, so the sebum creeps up through the follicle, onto the hair and out to the skin. Some sebaceous glands are situated on other, hairless parts of your body, and the sebum goes through a duct to get to the skin surface. Sebum is like a skin lubricant, but having too much or too little sebum can cause havoc.

Zit City

It always seems to happen on picture day at school. You wake up early that morning to get ready. You shower, do your hair and look in the mirror. There it is. A big ugly zit on your nose, staring right back at you. Ugh!

Pimples, pustules, zits—they are what happens when pores (the tiny holes in your skin) get blocked. Ever notice that nobody gets pimples on the palms of their hands or the soles of their feet? That's because there aren't any hair follicles with oil-producing sebaceous glands there. Oily sebum and dead skin cells can plug up a hair follicle and create a whitehead.

A blackhead is a plug that reached the surface and darkens. It's not dirt that causes it to turn black but a reaction with the air. Whitehead or blackhead, if the plugged up follicle walls break, bacteria gets in and makes the area red and swollen. That's a pimple, and sometimes it's big enough to be called a pustule (or a mini Mount Vesuvius!), ready to blow its top of pimply juice pus!

The Dreaded "A" Word

When pimples start popping up all over your face, neck and even your back, you've got acne. Anyone can get acne. Teenagers often have acne because hormones make their sebaceous glands run in overdrive. Adults may find that their skin breaks out when they are under stress. Even newborn babies sometimes get teeny tiny pimples all over their noses and cheeks because their skin oil glands are trying to sort themselves out.

Cystic acne is the really bumpy, red and swollen kind. The follicles deep within the skin break and become inflamed. Sometimes, they can leave scars. Special medications and creams can help with acne. Acne is partly hereditary (you inherit it from your parents), so eating too much chocolate, pizza or junk food doesn't cause acne.

Chicken Skin

Have a bunch of little bumpy zits on the back of your arms or your butt? Think it looks like chicken skin? It's keratosis pilaris and happens when the follicles on your skin in that area have too much keratin built up around them. Sometimes they look inflamed and itchy; sometimes they're just hard bumps— similar to goose bumps, but they don't disappear when you stop shivering.

YUCK!

The ancient Romans had a stinky solution for acne. They bathed in hot water full of minerals, such as sulfur, which, of course, stinks like rotten eggs.

Very Vulgar VERRUCA

You've just had your weekly swim lesson and are in the change room. You sit down on the bench, dry off and are about to put your socks on, when you notice something on the ball of your foot. It's a small, round, flat, brown spot surrounded by tender skin. You rub it, but it won't come off. When you press on it, it hurts. Congratulations. You are now the proud owner of a verruca vulgaris—a wart.

In this case, it's probably a plantar wart, which is usually found on the bottom of feet and can be painful to walk on. Other warts look like cluster growths or tiny cauliflowers. You're in sympathetic company if you get a wart; three out of four people have one. They often appear on the wrists, hands, knees and elbows but can pop up anywhere. Most warts look like little grayish brown cauliflowers with black dots in them. Others can be flat and pink, brown or yellow. You can even get finger-like warts around your mouth, eyes or nose.

Contrary to popular myth, you won't get warts if you touch a toad or a frog, or any other reptile. Warts are caused by a virus, the human papilloma virus (or HPV, which also causes warts on your "privates," but we'll get to that later). They can be single or in a bunch and are the most common skin complaint after acne. Warts usually go away on their own, but if they are bothersome, a doctor can remove them. Don't be embarrassed. You won't be the first, or the last.

GROSS!

You're in sympathetic company if you get a wart; three out of four people have one.

Wart Removal Through the Ages

10,000 BC

A caveman first shows interest in the wart on the back of his hand. Where did it come from? When will it disappear? No one knows, but his wife tells him to get back to hunting mammoths.

2300 BC

A favorite Egyptian musician dies. No one wants to remove his warts to prepare him for the "afterlife," so the warts are mummified along with his body.

400 BC

The Greek physician Hippocrates writes medical texts indicating that warts should be burned or cut out.

500 AD to 1500 AD

Superstition reigns supreme. Mixing pig poo with wood ashes is thought to cure warts. So is wearing a live toad in a bag around your neck until it dies. However, most people preferred a less smelly superstition to get rid of warts, such as making faces in a mirror at midnight for three nights in a row. If nothing else, it helped them to laugh about their warts.

1600 AD

Elizabethans have a great idea. They believe that rubbing a wart with a half-dead mouse helps (the wart, that is, not the mouse).

1700 AD

Everyone is afraid of witches, and witches have warts. The remedy? Burn the witches. That stops their warts, but not everyone else's.

1800 to 1900

Victorians obsessed with funerals come up with some new ideas. They rub the wart with a stone and then throw the stone after a hearse, chanting, "Wart, wart follow the corpse."

Today

Wart removal is big business. Among other cures are:

- squeezing (not ingesting) vitamin A or E oil onto the surface of warts

- smearing warts with ointments, lotions or pads that contain salicylic acid

- freezing warts with liquid nitrogen

- burning them off with a light electrical current

- using lasers to remove the warts

- using hypnosis or the power of suggestion to "wish" the wart away

And finally, there is the duct tape cure. Someone (probably a fan of the "Red Green Show") decided to cover a wart with duct tape and then forgot about it. Lo and behold, after while, the wart disappeared. Further tests reveal that leaving duct tape over a wart for three days at a time works best. Duct tape companies have yet to advertise this as a bonus to their product.

Well, I have this RASH...

The Rash: reddish or pinkish marks that appear on your skin. May be in one spot or all over your body, and can be itchy, irritated or inflamed. Is it a big deal? That depends. Sometimes, you know exactly why you have a rash. Other times, figuring out why this rash appeared on your skin is the same as trying to solve a mystery. Here are some examples of rashes and what to do about them.

I can't use that deodorant. It gives me a rash.

No big deal. The product has an ingredient your skin doesn't like. Discontinue using product.

Hey, I woke up with this fever and a rash all over my body!

Big deal. The rash may be a symptom of another condition or a disease. See a doctor.

Butt Rash

Diaper rash. That sore butt babies get. They pee and poop into a diaper and the result is high-pH environment that skin hates. Thankfully, Mom smears on some barrier cream to protect the sensitive skin or, if the baby promises not to have an accident, she'll let it crawl around in the buff. Nothing like fresh air to heal sore skin.

Itchy Ivy

Leaves of three, leave 'em be.

Guess what? Poison ivy isn't an ivy. It's actually a very nice type of woody vine, except for one thing—urishol—the poisonous oil that it produces. When urishol comes in contact with skin, most people get redness, inflammation, itchiness and blisters that can last about a week.

A Nickel Pickle

If you have pierced ears, or any pierced body part for that matter, you might have experienced nickel dermatitis. It's a type of contact dermatitis, a reaction your skin gets when something touches it that it doesn't like. You might even find that wearing your favorite piece of jewelry gives you a rash.

Breaking out in Hives

A hive is a raised patch of skin that resembles a mosquito bite. If it's an itchy rash, it's called urticaria. That irritating itch comes from the histamine your cells release as they try to get rid of the inflammation. The hives are caused by leaky capillaries, those tiny veins near the surface of your skin. Fluid seeps out and collects just beneath your skin.

People can get hives from allergic reactions (something they ate or touched, for example), an insect bite or sting, exposure to the cold or heat (heat rash) or even stress. You can also get hives from putting too much pressure on the skin. For instance, you may get a rash on your shoulder under the strap of a heavy knapsack. All the more reason to leave those textbooks in your locker!

Allergic to the Sun

"Solar" means "sun", and "urticaria" is another word for "hives." Solar urticaria is really rare, but it causes hives in people who are exposed to the sun. They are super sensitive to the UV wavelengths of the sun, which causes their skin to react. These unfortunate people are NOT related to vampires, though they may have been the inspiration behind part of that mythology.

Scary HAIRINESS

Believe it or not, humans are a very hairy species. On average, people have 20 million hairs on their body—and I'm not just talking about your uncle who entered the "hairy back contest" last year. Every one of us has more hair on our body than a gorilla, orangutan or chimpanzee! The reason we don't look as hairy as these animals (except for your uncle) is because human hair is much thinner and less noticeable than theirs. Of course, if our hair were similar to animal hair, we'd call it "fur" and save a huge amount of money on coats every winter.

Here a Hair, There a Hair

Humans have three types of hair on their bodies:

Scalp hair—the hair on our heads. Most of us like to style it, cut it, brush it or stick a baseball cap over it.

Terminal (or androgenic) hair—the hair found on beards, around your private parts, armpits, the upper lip and other places. This hair grows thicker and darker when hormones called androgens kick in around puberty (when you become a teenager).

Vellus hair—also called "peach fuzz." It doesn't change because of hormones the way terminal hair does. It's usually softer and all over the body, except for the palms of the hands and soles of the feet.

Scared Straight

Those tiny muscles attached at the base of the hair follicle are the arrector pili muscles. When you are cold, they pull the hair so that it stands up. When you're scared, these muscles might react the same way. Those are goose bumps, though they don't have anything to do with geese. But have you ever seen a plucked goose or chicken hanging in a butcher shop? Notice the bumpy skin. That's what goose bumps look like.

Do Blondes Have More Hair?

Match the average number of hairs on the head of each (natural) hair color:

a) 130,000 hairs

b) 110,000 hairs

c) 100,000 hairs

d) 90,000 hairs

1) brown

2) black

3) red

4) blonde

Answers: a) 4; b) 1; c) 2; d) 3

Stinky Scalp

Unfortunately, it is. We just can't smell our own scalp very often (our nose is in the wrong place for that). If you try to smell your brother or sister's scalp though, you'll see what I mean. It can stink. The scalp with all its hairs is the perfect breeding ground for yeast, and that produces the stinky scalp smell.

Those sebaceous glands are back at work. They produce natural oils and make our skin water-repellent. There is also a lot of sebum on your scalp. It creeps out of each hair follicle and spreads between the hairs and on them. The sebum starts to build up, and before you know it, you've got oily hair. Each strand of hair on your scalp can last up to five years, so if you never washed it you'd have stinky, sebum-covered hair!

A Different Kind of Hairball

Deep in the dark corners of certain stomachs lives a bezoar. Stomachs of this kind usually belong to goats or other cud-chewing animals. In medieval times, a bezoar was thought to be a cure for poisons. People carried stone-like bezoars around in their pockets as good luck charms in case they became sick. What was this mysterious creature? It wasn't a creature but a thing, a hardened mass of hair or plant fiber.

If a person frequently chews their hair, he or she can develop a trichobezoar, which is a fancy name for a bad hairball that can grow to the size of a chicken drumstick. The patient might vomit or feel full after eating even a small amount of food. However, the bezoar can't be puked up (like a cat does with a hairball), so a doctor has to operate on the patient to take it out. If most of the bezoar is in the stomach, but stringy parts of it extend into the middle of the small intestine, the patient has a problem called Rapunzel syndrome.

Dear Dr. Gross

My dad is losing his hair.
Is this going to happen to me?
I combed my hair this morning
and five hairs fell out.

Signed,
Hair Today, Gone Tomorrow?

Dear Hair:

I have good news…and I have bad news. The good news is that everyone loses about 100 hairs a day, so finding a mere few here and there is perfectly normal. The hair follicle, or little space in the dermis that grows each hair, can rest up to six months before it pushes up a new hair. Your dad's follicles, like those of many men, have "given up the ghost," I'm afraid, and that's why he's going bald. People can also lose their hair for all kinds of reasons: hormone changes, medications, chemotherapy. Hair loss can be permanent or temporary.

The bad news is that male baldness is hereditary. You may have the "lose-your-hair" gene. The other good news is you'll probably still be able to grow a beard and those long, lovely hairs that older people get—the ones that stick out of your nose and ears!

Remember the fairy tale about Rapunzel and her long hair? "Rapunzel, Rapunzel...let down your long bezoar..."

Unibrows

Have you ever wondered how many eyebrow hairs you'd need to pluck to get rid of an eyebrow? The answer is somewhere around 500 hairs. Double that, since most of us have two eyebrows. If you're lucky enough to have a Neanderthal-looking unibrow, or if SuperMario is your dad and Brooke Shields is your mom, then you might want to triple or quadruple that number. You could also wait the 10 weeks it takes for an eyebrow (or an eyelash) hair to fall out. Then again, that might not be such a great idea, because by that time, another has already taken its place!

Fuzzy Faces

Men grow beards, unless they shave, that is. Again, hormones are responsible for facial hair growth. A beard usually contains between 7000 and 15,000 hairs, and those are the fastest growing ones on the body. In his beard-growing lifetime, a man can spend over 3300 hours taking off that stubble.

If a guy never shaved, he could grow a beard up to 30 feet long! You may have seen your dad's beard stubble in the sink, but imagine if he had to shave a beard as long as a driveway. That would be one clogged drain. Not a desirable situation, unless you're a plumber.

Flaky Follicles

The hair follicles on our skin are sensitive critters and easily irritated. Occasionally, one might grow under the skin instead of out of it. It becomes an ingrown hair and traps bacteria that turns into an ugly, red, sore inflammation. Follicles don't like being tugged or cut by razors. That's why some people get little bumps on their skin after shaving. The ones that turn into pimples are called folliculitis.

Hyper Hairiness

"Bearded ladies" were often a sideshow in circus acts during the 19th and early 20th centuries. Many women have some facial hair, usually on their upper lip, but it's much finer than men's hair. Really hairy women have a condition called hirsutism, usually caused by hormones.

There is another, rarer condition called hypertrichosis, or the "werewolf syndrome." Some people with the severe form of this genetic condition grow hair on almost every part of the body, including their faces. It is so rare that there are only 19 people alive in the world today with severe hypertrichosis.

Hair Begone

Not an easy task. If you have too much hair in unwanted places, it can be embarrassing. Men don't seem to mind hairy arms, legs and backs, but say you're a woman with a light mustache. You can bleach it; that is, use a chemical to lighten the hair so it is not noticeable. You can shave it, but that usually creates a rough stubble and makes the hair look thicker. You can wax it off, which is like plucking out all the hairs at once. Or you can use a depilatory, which is a cream or lotion that dissolves the hair above the skin. In most cases, however, the hair grows back.

The only way to permanently remove the hair is by electrolysis, which kills the hair follicle with a tiny electric current. Lasers do the same thing over larger skin areas. Both are expensive treatments and must be done by professionals. Lastly, you could just learn to live with all your lovable, furry hairs!

Locks of White

Your hair is dead. Hanging dead stuff. The only "live" part of hair is deep within the hair follicle. That's why it doesn't hurt to cut your hair, or your fingernails and toenails. Hair turns silver, white or gray in older people because it loses its pigment. Can hair turn white overnight? If you saw that "Ten Commandments" movie, you might think so. In one scene, brown-haired Moses has a chat with God. Moments later, he returns with a head of white hair.

In reality, hair can't turn gray that quickly. The old, pigmented hair has to grow out, and that can take several months. People who actually lose their hair over a short period of time may have a condition called alopecia. If someone with partly grayed hair developed alopecia, and only the dark hairs fell out, it might look as though their hair turned gray suddenly.

Hair-Raising Records

According to the "Guinness Book of World Records," 50-year-old Radhakant Bajpai of India has the world's longest ear hair: one super-long strand sticks 5.19 inches out of his ear. And the world's longest recorded leg hair belongs to Tim Stinton of Australia. The hair on his left thigh is almost 5 inches long. Both of these men's hairs are about the same length as a hot dog!

Not So Dandy Dandruff
Snowflakes that land on my nose and eyelashes...

They also land on your hair, but when you've been in your nice warm house for the past hour and the snowflakes are still on your head, you know you've got a problem. Those white flakes are bits of dead skin from your scalp called dandruff. They hang around on your hair and clothes until they fall off and join the other skin flakes around the house and become...dust! That's right, most house dust is made of the human skin cells we constantly shed. So don't blame your dog for shedding. You do, too!

Belly Button Lint

Some people think belly buttons are rather gross by themselves. When you think of it, belly buttons are what's left over from a dried up, rope-like tube that looks like a telephone cord. It's a life-support tube, just like the ones that connect astronauts to their spaceships, except uglier.

Before you were born, you were attached to your mother's uterus (her womb) by a thick, springy tube full of blood called the umbilical cord. The stuff you needed to grow, such as nutrients from the food your mother ate, or the oxygen she breathed, came through that cord. When you came out of her womb so did the cord. Because you didn't need it anymore, the cord was tied close to your belly, then cut. It dried, shriveled up and became a dent in your belly called the navel or, as toddlers say, a belly button. Its concave shape makes it perfect for attracting lint, skin flakes, dust and other lovely things. If those bits and pieces stay there in that nice warm little cave, they start attracting bacteria and producing odors. Smelly belly button lint.

Buggy Eyelashes

Have you ever seen those false eyelashes in the makeup section of the drugstore? Well, just in case you decide to buy a pair because you want to have batty eyelashes for a New Year's party, think of this: When you glue them onto your real eyelashes, you're trapping the eyelash mites!

Yep, you are squishing tiny little creatures that eat, live and lay their eggs at the hair follicle base of most eyelashes!

Dear Dr. Gross

Today, my teacher sent me home with a note for my parents. It said head lice were found in our class. They didn't tell us where in the class they found the head lice. I guess someone saw lice on the floor, but why would they send home that note? Couldn't they just step on the bugs and kill them?

Signed,
Scratching My Head Over This

Dear Scratching:

Head lice are tiny bugs found on your scalp. You can get lice on any part of your body that has hair. Yep, that means, if you are old enough to have hair "down there" (around your privates), you could get lice there, too. Your school sent home that note because someone in your class has head lice and you could be next!

Are you really scratching your head a lot? Better take a look. Get under a bright light and ask someone to check your hair with a magnifying glass. Head lice suck your blood, and when they bite, they cause itching. They lay dark eggs, also called nits, that stick to the hair shaft. When the baby lice come out of their eggs, the shells look like white dandruff but stay on the hair. To get rid of lice, you have to use special shampoo, and then, with a fine-tooth comb, remove the eggs from each strand of hair. Now that's nit-picking work!

They are a kind of skin mite called a demodex mite. These mites love to eat the sebum, or oils, that comes out of the sebaceous glands. They are also found in hair follicles of the skin and scalp. You can almost hear them now, "Mite we have dinner on the eyelash tonight?"

DISGUSTING DEAD STUFF ON YOUR BODY

Bed Buddies

You might have heard this old saying:

Good night,

Sleep tight,

Don't let the bed bugs bite!

Sounds cute, doesn't it? The "sleep tight" part comes from the way beds were built back in the old days. They had ropes tied across the frame to hold the straw-filled mattress. People wanted their ropes "tied tight" so that their beds wouldn't sag. As for the bugs, well, they simply loved to hang out in the mattresses.

WOW!

If you kept every eyelash you grew in a lifetime and attached them end to end, you'd have almost 100 feet of eyelashes.

More Weird Bumps and LUMPS

Is it scabby? Swollen? Gunky or crusty? Does it look repulsive, flaky or just plain revolting? There's something on your skin, but what exactly is it? It's a confusing world out there. Here's the lowdown on some of the other ABCs of skin bumps, lumps and other problems.

Abscess A pocket of pus surrounded by skin or other tissue. It is red, hot and painful because all the blood is rushing there to fight off the infection. An abscess sometimes needs to be pierced or lanced so the pus or fluid can come out.

Bulla One humungous blister, filled with fluid. More than one are called bullae. "Bullous" means something that is blistery and fluid-filled.

Cyst A sac filled with fluid and lined with skin cells.

Dermoid Cyst A raised bump that's actually been there since birth and is filled with oily, yellowish gunk from the sebaceous glands and hair follicles.

Edema Swollen tissue or fluid that has collected just below the skin's surface.

Excoriation Basically, it's a scratch mark. Did your cat give you an excoriation? Naughty kitty!

Fissure A thin crack in the skin. It can appear on very dry skin, such as on your toes or the soles of your feet, or at the corners of your mouth. You can also get fissures in more embarrassing places, such as your butt hole (anal fissures) if the tissues tear slightly.

Gangrene The word comes from the Greek, meaning "a gnawed out sore." Dead tissue.

Hyperkeratosis Lots of scaly, dead cells on the surface of your skin.

Impetigo A bacterial skin infection that looks oozy, then crusty, like cold sores.

Keloid A clump of scar tissue that causes a raised lump.

Lesion A problem on the skin; for example, it can be an inflamed area, a bump, a tumor or just a pimple.

Macule A small, smooth area of the skin or a tissue where the color has changed.

Nodule A solid bump on the skin that is bigger than the eraser at the end of a pencil. Comes from the Latin word, "nodulus," meaning "a knot."

Papule One or more small, raised bumps on the skin.

Rosacea Reddened cheeks, nose and chin. Bad rosacea can have bumps or pimples. Santa Claus probably had rosacea on his cheeks and nose.

Scabies A mite (bug) that eats dead skin cells. It makes little tunnels right under the skin that itch like crazy.

Tag A hanging bit of skin that you can't remove easily. Is it a price tag? No, it's a skin tag.

Ulcer An open, oozing sore that can occur on the skin or even on an organ inside the body.

Vesicle An itty-bitty blister or small collection of fluid.

Wheal or Welt They both mean a swollen bump that can drive you crazy because it is so itchy, even if it only lasts for a few hours.

Xanthoma A yellowish pink sore spot in the eye.

Yaws A tropical disease that causes an infection in the skin, bones and joints, and can cause deformities.

Zit A pimple!

Marked From Birth

If you are born with a splotch on your skin, and it's harmless, that's a birthmark. These marks can, however, attract some rather stupid questions from people who don't know you well.

Question: Did you spill wine on your face?

Answer: No, I'm not as clumsy as you. If you MUST know, it's my port wine stain birthmark. I've had it since I was born.

Question: How did your daughter hurt her cheek?

Answer: She didn't. If you MUST know, it's her strawberry birthmark.

Question: I've never seen a brown patch of skin like the one on your arm. Looks like a coffee stain.

Answer: I don't even drink coffee, and even if I did, why would I let it stain my arm? If you MUST know, it's my birthmark!

Get out of Bed!

Think you'd like to stay in bed all day long, week after week, month after month? You might end up with a bedsore. People who are stuck in one position for a long time, such as in a bed, chair or wheelchair, are prone to these pressure sores, also called decubitus ulcers. Bedsores can show up on the ankles, back of the head, shoulder blades—anywhere skin and muscle get compressed or where there is rubbing or friction. Cells in the skin don't get the oxygen and nutrients they need and die off. The skin can get inflamed, blistered or infected. If bedsores aren't taken care of, they will get worse.

Say Wen?

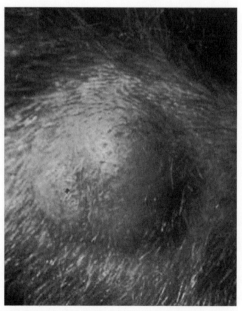

I have friend with a strange round bump on the top of his scalp. It looks as if an eraser from the end of a pencil was glued to his skin. When he started going bald and got a brush cut, the bump really stood out. Hairs never grew on it. When he'd ask me to buzz cut his head (number 0—"down to the wood"), I would be very careful around "the thing." I wasn't sure if I'd accidentally shave it off! What was it? A wen. A what? I know, it's a weird name. A wen is also called a pilar cyst and is found on the scalp or back of the neck. It's full of skin cells and, thankfully, isn't contagious!

Blistering Hot

Touch a hot stove and you'll get a blister. Hold your hand over the steam from a boiling kettle and you'll get a blister. Get a bad sunburn and you'll often break out in blisters. Yes, blisters are what happens when the skin gets a burn. They also come from friction and irritation, such as breaking in a new pair of shoes or shoveling without work gloves.

Really big blisters look like balloons on your skin that just ache to have the fluid drained from them. If they are pricked or break on their own, put on antiseptic ointment and keep them clean and bandaged. So the next time you buy new shoes, break 'em in with good, thick socks!

Bad Blisters and Beyond

First-degree burns hurt and make your skin red (sunburns, scalds).

Second-degree burns start to blister, ooze and hurt enough to make you cry.

Third-degree burns are white or cream-colored and often charred. They might not hurt because you've burned away the nerve endings, but you need to see a doctor because they can get infected.

Squished Skin

Ever pinch the skin on your finger between scissor handles or something similar? Ouch, that hurts! Often you're left with a little purple or dark red bump. That bump has blood in it, from a broken blood vessel under the skin. You've just given yourself a blood blister.

Fungus Is No Fun

Fungus is great if it's a mushroom. Not so great if it's the kind of fungus that creates itchy, red patches on your skin or under your nails. Fungus is like the mold on old bread or the mildew on shower tiles. It's really a microscopic plant. When it grows, it makes spores and then branches out. Yeast is a fungus, too, but its cells simply reproduce by dividing. One of the most common yeasts is candida fungus.

Like fungus, yeast cells have tough cellular walls that break through our thin human cells. Since they don't have stomachs to digest, fungus and yeast spew out enzymes that dissolve parts of our cells. Yep, that's how they eat our cells.

Bits of fungus and yeast are always on our skin and in our bodies, but they usually don't do any harm. Once in a while, under the right conditions, they go crazy and start reproducing too much. They crowd out our regular cells and can become a big problem. They can even weaken our immune system.

Because fungus and yeast cells can get deep into our tissues, we can't just brush a patch of them off our skin. Likewise, if there's fungus or yeast inside our bodies, it's hard to get rid of it. It's difficult, but not impossible. Medications have been developed that keep the critters in check. There are also some natural remedies, such as tea tree oil, that often help.

Gross Stuff "Down There"

Yep, skin flakes and oily secretions can collect in your, ahem, private parts. It's called smegma and is found in the skin folds of the body, especially ones that are warm, moist, and maybe not cleaned thoroughly, so bacteria thrive there. "Smegma" comes from the ancient Greek word for "soap," but unlike soap, human and animal smegma is whitish and smelly like bits of soft cheese.

Gruesome NAIL Tales

Animals and birds have claws, but we humans have nails! The root of your fingernail is hidden underneath the skin and grows from the matrix, which is an otherworldly place with nerves, blood vessels and lymph. Warp the matrix and you could end up with a deformed nail or one that won't grow back at all.

The nail bed also has blood vessels to bring nutrients to the nail. It's covered by the nail plate, that hard coating made of keratin, the same protein found in skin and hair. The nail bed keeps the plate together with natural oils, but if that dries up, nails can start to peel, crack or split. There's also a tiny half-moon at the base of your nail, it's the lunula ("moon"), but it doesn't glow at night.

Icky Down Under

Check out your nails. Yes, right now. When was the last time you trimmed them? Been a while, huh? There's a slew of gross stuff that collects under your nails. See that thin, black line between your nail and the skin? It's full of dead skin cells, dirt and other gunky stuff. You can scrub it with a nailbrush, or pick it out with a special nail instrument, but be careful. It will hurt if you pull back the area where the skin meets nail.

DISGUSTING DEAD STUFF ON YOUR BODY

Painful Nail Polish

If you hit your nail with a hammer, drop something heavy on your toenail, catch a finger in a door or damage your nail bed in any other way, blood vessels under your nail plate will bleed. You can develop a bruise that looks the same as purple or black nail polish, but it isn't. If the bruise is serious enough, you may have to wait until the nail grows out before it disappears. From the base to the tip, a finger-nail or toenail takes about six months to grow back completely. Your middle finger usually has the longest nail, and it's the one that grows the fastest. Toenails grow twice as slowly as fingernails. They're probably in no rush, since toes are constantly shoved into shoes anyway.

Tender Tootsies

When a nail, often the one on your big toe, starts to dig into the side skin, you've got an ingrown nail. You can get ingrown nails from damaging the nail or not cutting it straight across. Sometimes, if the nail cuts into the skin, it might get infected. In serious cases it can develop into a pus-filled, bloody or swollen bump that's major ugh!

CRAZY!

Lee Redmond of Utah is the "Queen of the Lady Fingers." She was in the "Guinness Book of World Records" for having the longest fingernails. Starting in 1979, she grew each nail to 33 inches, or more than 24 feet in total! She can do everyday things, such as cooking and cleaning, but when she dresses, she has to pull all her clothes up from the bottom. Ms. Redmond says that putting on a coat is one of the hardest things for her to do.

Foot FRENZIES

Your poor feet. Each foot has 38 bones, and they have to carry our weight, withstand pressure forces with every step, jog or jump we do, and more. No wonder they can look rather tired, wrinkly and dry. More than three-quarters of us have some kind of embarrassing problem with our feet. Maybe it's ugly, deformed toenails or gunk in between the toes. It could be scaly, hardened skin on the soles and balls of our feet, or perhaps they just stink to high heaven!

Corny Feet

Bunions, spurs and corns. They sound as if they're horseback-riding equipment, don't they? Except the last one, which reminds me of a yellow vegetable. Corns are yellowish, hardened spots often found on the top of toes. They're caused by friction or pressure, such as when you wear shoes that don't fit well. Bunions can be caused the same way. Bone or tissue sticks out at the base of the big toe or one of the smaller toes and can make walking painful. A spur is a bone growth on the heel. Like bunions, spurs can take years to develop, but when they do, ouch!

Stinky Feet

I used to love my high school theater arts class. We'd act out, improvise and even pretend we were tree branches swaying in the wind. But I hated actually going into the class. It was a small, carpeted room with no windows and one rule: Everyone had to take off their shoes. For eight hours a day, that synthetic nylon fiber floor was rubbed by two dozen pairs of sweaty socks. The room reeked and probably still does today.

Why do feet stink? Once again, the answer is sweat and bacteria. The skin on the soles of our feet is the thickest

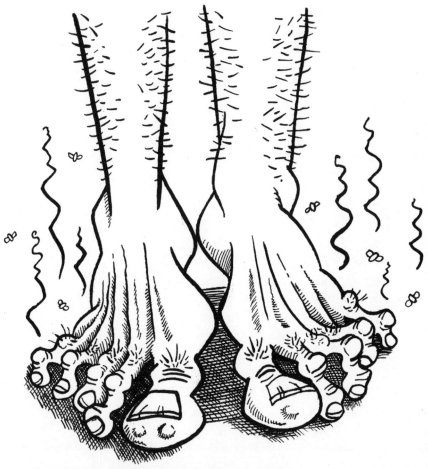

anywhere on the body, and it also has oodles of sweat glands, about 250,000 on each foot! In fact, there are more sweat glands on the hands and feet than anywhere else on the human body.

You've probably had sweaty palms, maybe when you were nervous or about to write a test. But hands are usually waving around in the air and most of the moisture evaporates. Bacteria don't like dry spots as much as moist ones. If you wore socks on your hands most of the day, they might start to smell, too, but most people don't do that. In our Western culture, most people do wear shoes and socks, and that causes problems.

Once bacteria are on your skin, they start having a field day. They eat away at the oils and dead cells they find there. After we eat, we excrete—and so do bacteria. Bacteria excrete chemical compounds that often have certain odors. When you smell stinky feet, you are actually smelling bacteria poop. One type of bacteria found on the feet is that old standby, brevibacteria. It produces bacteria poop that smells like stinky cheese. Have your sweaty gym socks or running shoes ever reeked of gross, old cheese? There you go.

DiD YoU KNOW?

Your foot is usually the same length as the distance between your wrist and your elbow.

Top Ten Reasons Why Your Feet Stink

10. You stepped in dog poo.

9. You don't trim your toenails and they get filled with gunk.

8. You have a skin disorder; go see a doctor.

7. You always wear the same shoes.

6. Your shoes are too tight.

5. You haven't taken your shoes off all day.

4. Your shoes are made of vinyl or synthetic material.

3. You hardly ever go barefoot.

2. You wear socks made of nylon or synthetic fabrics that don't "breathe" like cotton.

1. You don't wash and dry your feet (or socks)!

The key to preventing stinky feet is to keep them clean and dry. How? Switch shoes; wear shoes that aren't too tight; buy socks made of breathable fabrics that absorb sweat, such as cotton (not nylon or certain synthetics); remove your wet shoes or socks; and most of all, go barefoot or wear sandals whenever possible!

Athlete's Foot ... Not Just for Jocks

Athlete's foot is one nasty but common foot fungus. It's often found between the toes and can really drive you crazy with its itchy, scaly, red patches. If the skin becomes raw and exposed, it's prone to infection. The fungus that causes athlete's foot prefers to hang out in warm, moist, dark places, such as the inside of your shoes. You can also pick it up when you walk barefoot around swimming pools or the gym shower floor. That's why some people wear waterproof flip-flops in the changing rooms.

The fungus doesn't just affect your feet. It can also make your "privates" itchy. Yes, you can get athlete's foot in the groin area! Ewww! When you get it there, it's called jock itch.

To stop either one, you need to kill the fungus. You may have to wash your socks or underwear in super-hot water and put special antifungal cream on your infected skin for at least a month. Some people think that peeing on their feet will help get rid of athlete's foot fungus. That might be because of the urea found in urine, but this pee-pee treatment hasn't been proven yet. It also might gross out a lot of people in the gym showers.

Toe Jam and Cheese

Your little piggies collect the weirdest stuff between them—dust, bits of fibers from socks, dead skin cells. That's toe jam, and usually you can just flick it off in the shower or bath. When the gunk between your toes starts to smell, once again, blame it on bacteria. Feet, especially feet that are kept in moist, warm places (such as the inside of a sweaty sock nestled within a thick, synthetic running shoe) can start to grow all kinds of microscopic creatures. Many of the bacteria between your toes are similar to ones found in dairy products. No wonder we call it toe cheese! Just don't eat it.

GROSS "Birds & Bees" BITS

That Four-Letter Word Again ... YUCK!

Ah, the miracle of life. A cute and cuddly newborn nestled in the loving arms of Mr. and Mrs. Happy Couple. Is there anything more wonderful in the world? WARNING: The process by which that sweet little baby got here may be enough to make you gag!

Yes, that baby was once YOU, and when you find out how you got from nothing to a somebody, you'll never be the same again. It's even a scarier thought when you realize your parents and grandparents also went through this. Ugh! Once, like you, they were an ordinary boy and an ordinary girl until they hit a proverbial brick wall called puberty. They passed through it fine, but they can never go back. And it was all because of hormones.

Raging Hormones

There are chemicals inside of you. Oodles of them. Hormones are chemicals that act like tiny technicians to help regulate the body's functions. Each person has more than 100 of them, controlling everything from growth to digestion to how we react in certain situations.

Some organs, such as the pancreas, produce hormones, but the "hormone manager of the year" is the pituitary gland.

It's a pea-sized gland that sits at the base of your brain and releases at least nine important hormones. For instance, there's the "thrill hormone," also called adrenaline, which kicks in when you are doing things such as riding a roller coaster or skydiving.

Then there are the sex hormones that the gland triggers at puberty. Puberty happens somewhere between the ages of 8 and 18, lasts for a few years, and causes major growth changes in the body. Every adult you know has been through puberty. If they didn't, well, they'd all still look like kids!

Souped-Up on Steroids

Besides hormones, our body also produces steroids to help it function properly, but they can also be made artificially for use in medical treatments. Similar to the natural male hormone "testosterone," some artificial or anabolic steroids build muscle and increase strength. Some athletes and bodybuilders have been known to take these steroids. They call them "roids," "juice" and even "gym candy."

The side effects of taking steroids can be very dangerous. In females, their voice deepens, their boobs (breasts) disappear, and they grow facial hair. In males, steroids can make their balls (testicles) shrink or cause their breasts to develop. The girl starts looking like a guy, and the guy literally becomes a "girlie-man"!

Girls Go First

Did you ever notice that a lot of girls are taller than boys in grades six, seven and eight? That's because girls usually hit puberty before boys. Here's what happens to a girl during puberty:

- She grows taller.

- Her hips broaden.

- Her breasts start to develop.

- She grows more hair on her body, including pubic and underarm hair.

- She might want to start shaving her legs.

- She starts her period (menstruation).

Boys Catch Up

When boys go through puberty, they really catch up and overtake the girls. Here's what a boy goes through during puberty:

- He grows taller.

- His shoulders broaden.

- He grows more hair on his body, including pubic and underarm hair.

- He grows facial hair, downy at first, then coarse enough to have to start shaving.

- His genitals grow bigger.

- His testes start to produce sperm.

- His body becomes more muscular.

- His voice deepens because his larynx (voice box) grows larger.

Now who wants to go through all that? Isn't it much more fun to simply be a kid? Puberty isn't easy. It can be downright embarrassing at times. Not only does your body change, but your mind does, too. The ways you think and feel as teenager, and then as an adult, are different than how you felt as a child. It's a good thing, too, otherwise you wouldn't exist! The whole story is rather squeamish and involves a "tadpole" and an "egg."

The Story of the Tadpole and the EGG

Part I: The "Egg" Story

If you're a boy reading this, say, in your school library, you'll probably notice a few girls sitting around you. DON'T LOOK NOW, but perhaps one or more of those girls has their period. DON'T STARE; IT'S NOT POLITE. That's right. They don't want you to know, but they are shedding the old womb lining. In our culture, we hide that fact, but in other cultures, parents celebrate it with parties, cakes and cookies. They let EVERYONE know that their little girl is becoming a woman.

What happened? Girls are born with a womb (a pear-shaped organ in the lower abdomen also known as the uterus) with two ovaries, one on each side. Each ovary is smaller than your thumb, but even from birth they contain thousands of eggs, or ova. Somewhere around the age of 12, give or take a few years, girls start to menstruate, also known as "having a period," "that time of the month" or "being on the rag." It is sometimes even called "the curse," because it involves messy blood and the occasional cramps. No fun.

Once a month, an egg breaks out of its follicle (a little fluid bag in the ovary) and drifts down a thin tube (called the fallopian tube) to the womb. If the egg doesn't get fertilized, then the blood-rich lining of the uterus is shed through the vagina (a stretchy tube also called the birth canal). That's what a period is. Period. And you can blame the whole thing on hormones, again.

Part II: The "Tadpole" Story

At puberty, a human male's testicles (those two egg-shaped balls) produce special cells with squirmy tails. Under a microscope, these cells look just like tadpoles and are called sperm. They are made in long, coiled tubes called seminiferous tubules. Thousands of sperm cells are churned out every second—about 200 million each day.

In the testes (testicles), the sperm first look like blobs, which are called spermatocytes. They hang around for about 10 weeks until they've grown tails and feel mature enough to join the swim club. Sperm cells are the only cells in the human body with their own little swim propellers, called flagella. Without these flagella, they'd probably just become couch potatoes and sit around the testes drinking cold beer and watching sports.

Speaking of cold, the reason all this sperm-making happens outside the body, in the scrotum, is because it's cooler there. Sperm don't like the average body temperature of 98.6°F. They prefer it when the heat is turned down.

Eventually, the sperm will come out of the urethra as semen. The urethra is the tube in the penis that also carries urine to the outside of the body. Semen is a thick, liquid goop that looks the same as hair conditioner, but it isn't. Semen's destination is to meet a woman's egg, and that means it has to get into a woman's body.

Dear Dr. Gross

A couple of times a week I wake up with sticky stuff on my bed sheets. I think it came from my private parts. I'm so embarrassed. Will it come out in the wash?

Signed,
Will It?

Dear Will:

It will, and I am sure your parents will understand. You probably had a nocturnal emission, also known as a wet dream, and the stuff on your sheets is the ejaculate. This usually happens to boys between the ages of 12 and 15, and it isn't always related to sexy dreams. Only about 60 percent of men have had nocturnal emissions in puberty. The rest, well, they're awake when these things happen, and they often bring it on themselves, if you know what I mean (it's called masturbation).

GROSS "BIRDS & BEES" BITS

Part III: Tadpole Meets Egg (Sort of)

How the tadpoles (sperm) get to the egg, the old-fashioned way, is that sperm comes out of a man's penis and goes into a woman's vagina—it's called sexual intercourse, or "sex" for short. Although kids may think that's gross, most adults see it in an entirely different light (especially if it's candlelight). And that's a good thing, because if they didn't, nobody would bother making babies and, well, the human race would just fade away.

So the tadpoles swim their hearts out up the vagina and through the fallopian tubes. Their mission? To meet the egg and ram right into it. Once one tadpole succeeds, it chemically lets all the others know that they've lost the race. For them, it's game over, but for the egg that just got fertilized, it's a whole new beginning.

Baby Beginnings

For half an hour or so after the sperm enters the egg, the now fertilized egg is a zygote. It sounds like a creature from a science-fiction movie, but just remember that every human, including you, was one once! There are 46 chromosomes—23 from the egg and 23 from the sperm in this first cell, which is YOU now.

Within those chromosomes is DNA, which contains genes. Whether you have blue or brown eyes, curly or straight hair, and all sorts of other characteristics, depends on which genes in your DNA you inherited from your parents. Unless you have an identical twin, everyone has a certain arrangement of DNA that's slightly different. It's your genetic fingerprint.

The zygote then starts to divide and turns into a hollow ball of cells called a blastocyst. It keeps on dividing and dividing as if there were no tomorrow while it attaches to the uterus wall. It turns into an embryo, and after about four weeks is as tiny as an apple seed. Eight weeks later, it's called a fetus and is as big as a grape. The fetus floats in a watery liquid called amniotic fluid, the liquid that's inside the amniotic sac within the womb. If you could see the fetus, you'd be able to make out fingers, toes, eyes and all sorts of other human features. At three months, the fetus even has fingerprints. The fetus keeps growing until nine months are up and, just like a cooked Thanksgiving turkey, it's ready to come out!

The Test-Tube Baby

Every three seconds, a human egg is fertilized somewhere around the world. A select few of these fertilizations happen in a test tube, called "in vitro fertilization" (IVF). The first "test-tube baby" was Louise Brown in 1978. She is now all grown-up with a baby of her own.

The Baby Pool

The watery amniotic fluid surrounding the baby isn't your typical baby swimming pool. It contains proteins and other compounds but is mostly urine—yes, baby pee. No wonder babies like to pee in the bathtub! While in the womb, the baby actually practices breathing by taking amniotic fluid in and out of his or her lungs. Before they are born, babies are covered in downy, fine lanugo hairs. These hairs fall off before birth and swish around with other old cells in the amniotic fluid. So, in a way, the baby actually sucks in all that hair, too!

The Pregnant Man

Can men get pregnant? Well, in 1999, a 36-year-old man in India who was rushed to the hospital certainly looked pregnant. And in a sense, he was. Before he was born, he shared his mother's womb with another fetus—his identical twin. Except his twin never really developed into a person the way he did. Instead, it attached to his stomach and grew into a mass of flesh inside him. It used the man's blood supply for food and oxygen but eventually started to give its host (the man) medical problems.

When doctors operated on the man, they took out what was left of the fetus: some bones, limbs, fingernails and hair. The man was relieved that his stomach pain was gone and that he didn't look pregnant anymore. This condition, called "fetus in fetu," is very, very rare, but it did happen!

What's an STI?

Could it be pasta sauce? Of over 1000 people polled in Great Britain, nearly two-thirds thought "arrabiata" was a sexually transmitted infection, or STI. Arrabiata is actually an Italian spicy tomato sauce. The survey, which was released on World AIDS Day in 2006, was done to find out how much people knew about STIs.

An STI is spread by sexual contact—someone else's private parts touch your private parts. STIs are sometimes referred to as sexually transmitted diseases (STDs), and years ago, they were called venereal diseases. Either way, they can be caused by bacteria, viruses or even a one-celled animal called a protoza. STIs are often ugly, itchy, infected, full of pus, and sometimes people with STIs don't have any symptoms. It all depends on the type of STI. The most common is the human papilloma virus (HPV). There are many different types of HPVs; some cause those nuisance warts on fingers and feet, but others actually infect your "privates." Nobody wants warts there. And there is no cure for HPV or STIs such as herpes, hepatitis B and HIV.

Other STIs are curable if they are treated quickly. Chlamydia is one STI that many people don't know they have. Medications can prevent it from damaging reproductive organs and causing infertility. Gonorrhea and syphilis are STIs that have been around for centuries. King Henry VIII, the famous King of England who had six wives, and many more girlfriends, was said to have had syphilis when he died. In its later stages, syphilis actually makes the sufferer go insane.

Disgusting from Day ONE

Childbirth

is a baby being born. It can involve screaming, sweating, crying, blood, poop and other bodily fluids. That said, if you ask most adults about the day baby meets world, they'll tell you it's a wonderful experience. Afterwards, of course. The process usually starts with labor pains. They are strong muscular contractions in the mother's womb that tell her body it's time to get the baby out.

Then the "water breaks," and amniotic fluid might gush out. The baby's head pushes down through a space (the cervix) about four inches in diameter and out the vagina into the world.

Newly born babies come out wet and are often covered in greasy, creamy white stuff called vernix. When the baby was in the womb, the vernix protected the baby's skin from getting water-logged. After the birth, the baby is cleaned up, along with all the crap that came out, too. Then the baby is wrapped in a warm blanket or towel and looks just like a picture from one of those "Congratulations On Your New Baby" cards.

Mama's Milk

When you were a newborn, you cried. You were probably hungry, so one of two things was stuck in your mouth—

a bottle nipple or a real-life breast nipple. Yes, unless you were fed baby formula, you were likely breastfed by your mother. I know, it's not something you want to think about, but breast milk has always been the best nourishment for a baby. It contains the right amount of ingredients for an infant's growth. Some women even donate their breast milk to premature babies in hospitals. Human breast milk is that important for babies.

Once again, hormones are what set off the "Mommy Milk Production" a few months after your mother became pregnant. Little sacs, or glands, in her breasts slowly grew and got ready to produce milk. After birth, these glands, called milk ducts, turned on the milk tap. The "milk" first came out as colostrum, a thick, yellow fluid full of antibodies to help keep the baby healthy during those first few days, and later became mature milk.

Placenta Spaghetti

The placenta is a temporary organ that gives food and oxygen to the baby from the mother's blood. It's attached to the baby through a thick, cable-like cord called the umbilical cord, and everything goes through it. The placenta is also called the afterbirth because it follows the baby "after the birth."

Depending on what the parents want to do with the placenta, it's either thrown away or, umm, taken home. Animal mothers often will eat the placenta, but not a lot of humans do, which is not to say that NO ONE does. A few people actually eat it—that's called placentophagy. Apparently, you can chop it up to make placenta spaghetti or some other recipe. Again, most people DO NOT do this! In some cultures, parents take the placenta home and plant it under a tree as a birth ritual. The tree is watched as it grows, along with the baby. Ahhh.

The Nastiness never ENDS

So far, this book has covered gross things about the human body. But there's more! If you thought the living human body was gross, just wait until you find out what happens after your body takes its last breath and heartbeat. It will happen to us all, eventually. For most of us, that day is far off in the future. No need to worry about it now. There are more people alive today than have ever died in human history. That should continue for quite some time. But somewhere, somehow and sometime, death will knock at your door. What happens next is the ultimate in yucky, the ubergross, and is a fact—the last one—of life.

Dead as a Doornail

What is "dead"? Is it when your heart or your brain stops working? Doctors have determined it's when someone is brain-dead—that is, when no activity can be registered in the brain. None of the usual electrical zaps occur. A machine (electroencephalogram, or EEG) that monitors electrical activity in the brain produces a flat line that can't be reversed. That's the official definition of death in most countries.

Of course, if your brain dies but your heart and lungs are kept going by artificial machines, your healthy organs (heart, eyes, lungs, kidneys and so on) could be donated to someone who needs them. It's not unlike the time my car needed a new window because the original one was smashed. I phoned a few autowreckers to see who had one in stock. I found one, and voilá, a replacement window for my car was taken from an old, broken-down one. Organ donation, of course, is much more complicated and serious, but essentially, a dead person's organs live on in another human being. It's the ultimate gift.

Off With Your Head!

What if your brain is the last to know that you're dead? It's a scary thought. Let's go back to the late 18th century, when the preferred method of execution in France (especially during the French Revolution) was the "national razor"—the guillotine. With its sharp, heavy blade that quickly dropped several feet onto a victim's neck, it was supposed to be a painless method of beheading. By 1794, even the man for whom the device was named, Dr. Joseph-Ignace Guillotin, worried that perhaps the decapitated heads were momentarily aware of what had happened. In 1905, a Dr. Beaurieux did an experiment. After a prisoner named Henri Languille had his head chopped off, Beaurieux called out the victim's name:

"I called in a strong, sharp voice, 'Languille!' I saw the eyelids slowly lift up...Next, Languille's eyes very definitely fixed themselves on mine and the pupils focused themselves.... I was dealing with undeniably living eyes that were looking at me. After several seconds, the eyelids closed again, slowly and evenly, and the head took on the same appearance as it had had before I called out. It was at that point that I called out again and, once more, without any spasm, slowly the eyelids lifted and undeniably living eyes fixed themselves on mine with perhaps even more penetration than the first time... I attempted the effect of a third call; there was no further movement and the eyes took on the glazed look which they have in the dead."

Was the beheaded prisoner reacting and thinking? He never said a word, but then again, his vocal chords were probably still with his headless body.

Once a person truly does die, there's no turning back. At least not yet, anyway. What first happens to the body is called pallor mortis. Your skin gets very pale because the blood has stopped circulating. Your brain, heart and lungs all stop, and your body goes limp. Body cooling, or algor mortis, then begins. The muscles in your body relax, so some gas might escape (in other words, you could fart). You could pee a bit (it leaks out) or even dribble some poo.

Dear Dr. Reaper:

What is the worst way to die? I say it's being mauled to death by a lion or bear. My friend thinks that being thrown in a vat of acid like the bad guys in those spy movies is worse. What's your opinion?

Signed,
Curious Chums

Dear Curious:

Both seem equally unpleasant. Accidents are always nasty ways to go, especially if there is the possibility the person feels pain or is aware that he or she is dying. When a doctor lists a "cause of death," it is usually due to an illness, a natural cause, a murder (homicide) or an accident. There are probably countless ways to die. No one really knows which "manner of death" is worse because no one has come back to say, "I'd give that death an 11 on a scale of 1 to 10!" or something to that effect. However, dying in your sleep might be one of the better ways to go but who knows? For the living, it's still a mystery.

It all depends on the way you die and your last actions in life, but that's the general idea.

Your internal body temperature goes down, so if someone touched your skin, it would feel cool. The blood in your body then starts to drain down to the lowest point, depending on gravity. It leaves purplish red splotches on the skin and is called lividity (livor mortis). Parts of the body that are in contact with the ground or have an object pressed on them don't get this discoloration, because the tiny blood vessels have been squished and can't fill up with blood.

After a few hours, chemical changes in the muscles cause them to stiffen. This is the beginning of rigor mortis. It starts in the smaller muscles, such as the eyelids, fingers and toes, and builds up to the bigger muscles. Eventually, the whole body is one big "stiff." Rigor mortis eventually subsides, and the body goes into decomposition. That's the process that eventually turns you into a skeleton. If you're not embalmed or preserved in some way, decomposition usually takes a few months (or a few days if you're out in the open and there's a heat wave).

Back to Goo

One of the first signs that your body is decomposing is a greenish tinge in the skin around the abdomen a day or two after death. The green color spreads throughout the body because of the chemical reactions going on inside. Unless you are kept in a cold environment (such as a refrigerated morgue), your cells break down in a process called autolysis. Enzymes in your body start to eat through your cells, and the liquid inside these cells leaks out.

Bacteria, that were always present, start feeding and multiplying, too. This time, they're not munching away on food—they're eating you! That produces gas, as usual, but this time, the gas doesn't escape. Instead, it builds up in the body. Left alone, a dead body starts to bloat, like a balloon. Most parts bloat and bulge outwards. The dead body bloats for about a week, as it turns from green to purple to black. This is putrefaction, from which we get the word "putrid," which describes a very gross smell. In fact, a dead body gives off two not-so-lovely chemicals during decomposition. They are putrescine and cadaverine. You won't find these chemicals on the perfume shelves anytime soon, because they stink beyond belief.

While the bacteria work away, body tissues turn to liquid. Everything starts to disintegrate and liquefy. This slimy, bloodstained goo seeps out of the mouth, nose, anus and other body orifices, and the brain get squishier. After about a week, goop from the cells gets into the skin and lifts it off in big sheets. It's called "skin slip," because the skin can actually slip off if touched. When all the muscles and organs have dissolved, not much is left except a skeleton and a yellowish ooze that looks like chicken soup gone bad. Since they are so hard, bones can last a long time. Maybe even long enough for an archaeologist to dig them up!

Maggot Buffet

Bug, insects, creepy crawlies and especially maggots are actually very important when it comes to decomposition. They feed on dead things, including dead people. You've probably seen roadkill covered in flies on the side of the highway. Insects, such as the blowfly, lay their eggs on dead tissue so that their young, the maggots, can feed. Scientists can find out how long a body has been left outside by the age of the maggots and the number of maggots on the body.

Goodbye... for GOOD?

If you visit a funeral home, the dead person you see has been embalmed. That's the process in which blood is flushed out and replaced with special embalming fluid. Chemicals, including formaldehyde, are injected into the blood vessels and internal organs to stop decay, at least temporarily. The mortician, or funeral home worker, makes sure the dead person's eyes stay closed and the jaw doesn't hang open. A stitch or two might be sewn into the mouth just to make sure it doesn't suddenly yawn in the middle of the eulogy. The hair is cleaned and arranged. Foundation makeup and a hint of blush or lip color is applied. Nobody wants an embalmed corpse to appear gray and lifeless. The point of all this is to make the corpse appear as if asleep.

Embalming only became popular in the last century. Famous embalmed people include Russia's Vladimir Lenin (preserved through

GROSS!

When Pope Pius XII died in 1958, a bad embalming job left him decomposing while lying in state. Swiss Guards stationed around his body fainted from the stench, the pope's skin turned black and his nose actually fell off.

ongoing special embalming), and Eva Peron, the wife of the Argentine president Juan Peron. The process grew in popularity in the West after President Abraham Lincoln was embalmed. Before then, when you died, you didn't look as though you were taking a nap. You looked dead, very dead.

Getting Rid of the Body

After people die, their bodies are either cremated or buried. During internment or burial, the body is usually placed in a coffin or casket and buried. In some cultures, a cloth, called a shroud, is placed over the body. Either way, the body will eventually decay.

Another way to dispose of a body is by cremation. Some religions insist that a corpse be cremated rather than buried. The body is burned at a very high temperature until only a few pounds of charred bone bits remain. In a few hours, most of the body has literally been vaporized into the air. The bone fragments may then be ground up, placed in an urn or special box and returned to the family as cremated remains (cremains) or ashes.

Soap Mummies

When the conditions are right (namely, not much air), some corpses go through a process called adipocere formation. They actually turn...soapy! Another name for the process is saponification, which means making a fat into a soap. What happens is that anaerobic bacteria convert the body fat to adipocere, a process that drastically slows down the decomposition of many tissues and organs.

Because of their high body fat content, babies who have died sometimes go through adipocere formation. The next time you walk through a modern graveyard, think of this. Many of the embalmed corpses in modern, air-tight caskets below the ground today probably have some adipocere formation. If the bodies were to be exhumed (dug up from their graves), they would look remarkably well preserved, but would definitely not have that healthy glow.

Who's My Mummy?

Every once in a while, you hear a news story about a person found mummified in his or her home. No one bothered to check on the person for years, until an unfortunate soul makes the gruesome discovery. Mummification is the process of preserving the body. The Egyptians practiced mummification for over 3000 years. They did it because they believed the soul needed the body in the afterlife. At first, they stuck the bodies in hot sand, which soaked up the corpse's fluids. The organs and skin became preserved, but they were also quite dark and hardened, not very life-like at all.

Ancient civilizations in Chile also mummified their dead, using mud, but they may have done this in order to keep the bodies around to help them with their grief rather than for an afterlife. The Incans of Peru were known to take sacrificed children high up in the mountains for the gods.

A Human Popsicle

Extreme cold can also mummify bodies. In 1991, a 5300-year-old body was found by tourists in the Italian Alps. This iceman, whom scientists called Ötzi, had died in a small area that had quickly frozen over. It was as if his body had been kept in a freezer for thousands of years; he was well preserved and even had his tools with him. Ötzi, the human Popsicle, was a natural mummy.

Bog Man

He's not the bogey man, but he sure looks as though he could be. Lindow Man is one of thousands of "bog bodies" that have been found in the swampy peat-moss bogs of Europe. Most seemed to have died violent deaths—they were either executed or ritually sacrificed. When Lindow Man was found in England in 1984, he was so well preserved that scientists could even identify his last meal—cereal grains.

Die Another Day

Would you like your liver to live on forever, at least in some form? How about a kidney or a chunk of your brain? What about your entire body? Plastination involves turning all of your cells into a polymer, or special plastic. Bacteria don't like to feed on plastic, so decomposition is stopped.

The body, or body part, is embalmed, then soaked in acetone (essentially nail polish remover). The acetone is then removed through a vacuum and the body part is dipped in a special liquid polymer. Once hardened, it becomes a rigid plastic. Plastinated body parts look very realistic, because they are real. Many are used by medical schools to teach anatomy. One entrepreneurial German doctor who perfected the technique actually turns entire bodies into plastic-like human sculptures and tours them in international exhibitions. What a way for a body to "see" the world (if only it could!).

Cold as Ice

But what if you could preserve your body with the hope that one day it could come back to life? That's the idea behind cryonics. Your body is frozen after death so it won't decompose. Then, months, years, maybe even centuries later, you are "warmed up" and "brought back to life." Being frozen can cost over $100,000. You could just have your head frozen in the hope that when they do bring you back to life, you'll have a brand new body. That's cheaper.

Unfortunately, there are no guarantees that you'll come back. Experiments to thaw frozen mammals haven't been very successful. That's because cells contain water, and when they freeze, they expand like an ice cube. In the case of cells, they explode. Frozen frogs have been defrosted in a laboratory. And in one report, a tree frog found in a walk-in freezer in an Australian cafeteria was apparently successfully revived by the sympathetic lady who found it. As for people, it hasn't happened—yet.

There are, however, medical cases of young children, apparently dead and stiff (as if frozen), who do come back to life. In February 2001, an 18-month-old toddler in Edmonton, Alberta, wandered outside one night. When she was found, her body temperature was half what it should have been. Doctors managed to get her heart beating again, and she recovered. Seven years earlier, a two-year-old Saskatchewan girl was found outside in the middle of the night. Six hours later, she was "frozen stiff." She, too, was brought back to life, though she lost a leg from frostbite.

Self-Preserved

Sometimes, a body doesn't seem to decompose. Various religions have examples of holy men and women whose bodies are still preserved despite any human intervention such as embalming. They are called incorruptible. In the Catholic Church, the bodies of some saints, such as St. Bernadette of Lourdes, who died in 1879, can still be viewed. May the saints preserve us!

Mummy-Making

The ancient Egyptians believed that people needed their bodies in the afterlife. How did they preserve those who had died? Here's a step-by-step guide:

First, get an iron hook, stick it through the nose, and remove the brain, piece by piece (the ancients didn't think it was necessary to keep the brain). Second, carefully cut out all the other organs and put most of them in special jars. Leave the heart inside the body, because that's an important one. Stuff the body with incense and cloths. Dry it out in a special place where animal scavengers won't pick at it. Cover the body with a salty powder called natron and leave it there for a long time. Once dry, restuff the inside of the body with more natron and linen. Tightly bandage the body with long strips of cloth. Coat the body in hot plant resins so everything "glues" into place. After wrapping the mummy, place it in a special coffin and give it a decorated mask that looks just like the person did when he or she was alive.

In the Name of Science

Hey, anyone can end up in medical school—if they donate their body to science. Sign on the dotted line, and you agree to have your body, or parts of it, used for research or to teach medical students. It's an unselfish act, considering that millions of people have benefited from the knowledge. Most medical institutions will even give you a free cremation when they are finished with you. But it hasn't always been easy to work on human corpses.

In 300 BC, King Ptolemy I of Egypt ruled that it was OK to dissect human bodies, but by the Middle Ages in Europe, the practice wasn't encouraged. Most people believed in resurrection after death. Naturally, they didn't want their bodies left in pieces, because that might complicate the afterlife situation. Dissection was only allowed on executed criminals.

In England during the 1800s, there was often a shortage of bodies for medical science. Some people became grave-robbers and stole bodies from graves to sell to medical schools. These people were "body snatchers." There was a famous British case in which two men, William Hare and William Burke, secretly murdered more than 20 people and sold their bodies for anatomy study. Both men were caught, but only one was convicted—he was hanged and ended up dissected on a table, just like his victims!

The future of GROSS

There

is no escaping the gross and disgusting aspects to our bodies...or is there?

Perhaps, one day in the future, people simply won't have to worry about embarrassing smelly feet or putrid pus. In a way, we are now headed in that direction. We have antiperspirants and deodorants to put the brakes on body odor. Special shampoos get rid of dandruff or oily scalps. You can already buy products to dissolve stomach and intestinal gas so you don't fart or burp as much. What's next? A pill to make the farts you do have smell like roses?

If we are in a war against gross, it might be science that one day discovers the ultimate weapon. We now know the key to long life is in that giant library within our cells, our DNA. It's the damage to our DNA that makes us age. If science can alter that, we can potentially live much longer. Maybe science can also genetically alter DNA so all the gross aspects to our bodies are much more pleasant.

Imagine, no more boogers, bloodshot eyes or bad breath. If they pop up at all, wrinkles, welts and warts just as quickly miraculously disappear. Poop and pee are designer purple, pink or whatever pretty color and fragrance you want them to be. Heck, science might even find a way for humans to never have the need to excrete, fart or burp ever again.

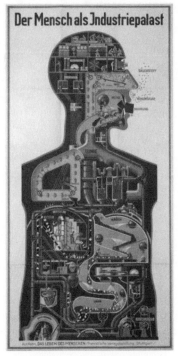

Der Mensch als Industriepalast

Hmm, on second thought...that could take away all the fun!

Other Places to find out about GROSS stuff

There are many great resources for learning more about the gross and disgusting things about the human body. The Internet, including websites such as wikipedia.com, answers.com, eurekascience.com or howstuffworks.com, is a good place to start, though as with most information on the Internet, don't assume everything you read is accurate. Dig further to make sure the facts are correct.

Other websites:

http://www.kidzworld.com/site/p473.htm

http://www.sciencemuseum.org.uk/exhibitions/grossology/indexflash.asp

http://www.yucky.discovery.com/body

Sources used in research for this book:

Clayman, Charles, ed. **The Human Body: An Illustrated Guide to its Structure, Function and Disorders.** London: Dorling Kindersley, 1995.

Elfman, Eric. **Almanac of the Gross, Disgusting & Totally Repulsive**. New York: Random House, 1994.

Elliott, Lynne. **Medieval Medicine and the Plague.** New York: Crabtree Publishing Company, 2006.

"Eye-Blowing Bubbles." Interview with Kenneth Keith. Personal conversation with the author. www.kennethkeith. com.

"Farty pants' set to cause a stink." http://www.metro.co.uk/news/article.html?in_article_id=34062&in_page_id=34 (accessed January 21, 2007).

"Gross in the News." Source: Reuters, October 13, 2006.

Marsh, Carole. **Official Guide to Germs.** Peachtree City, GA: Gallopade International, 2003.

Parker, Steve. **Digestion and Reproduction.** Understanding the Human Body series. Milwaukee, WI: Gareth Stevens Publishing, 2005.

Parker, Steve. **Skin, Muscles, and Bones.** Understanding the Human Body series. Milwaukee, WI: Gareth Stevens Publishing, 2005.

Roach, Mary. **Stiff: The Curious Lives of Human Cadavers.** London: W.W. Norton & Co., 2003.

Rogers, Kristeen, and Henderson, Corinne. **Human Body.** London: Usborne Internet-Linked Library of Science, Usborne Publishing, 2001.

Spinard, Paul. **The Re/Search Guide to Bodily Fluids**, San Francisco: Research Publications, 1994.

Treays, Rebecca. **Understanding Your Muscles & Bones.** London: Usborne Publishing, 1997.

Walker, Richard. **Human Body**. London: Dorling Kindersley, 2001.

http://dmd.aspetjournals.org/cgi/content/full/29/4/539

http://dopamine.chem.umn.edu/chempedia/index.php/Stomach_Acid#Why_doesn.E2.80.99t_the_stomach_digest_itself.3F

http://drgreene.healthology.com/teen-health/article1429.htm

http://en.wikipedia.org/wiki/Nose-picking

http://faculty.washington.edu/chudler/tt.html

http://in.news.yahoo.com/040411/139/2ci0w.html

http://www.aafp.org/afp/20060715/photo.html

http://www.science.edu.sg/ssc/detailed.jsp?artid=16&type=6&root=4&parent=4&cat=42

http://www.abc.net.au/spark/smelly/begone/begone02.htm

http://www.abcnews.go.com/Primetime/story?id=2346476&page=1

http://www.bl.uk/catalogues/illuminatedmanuscripts/GlossP.asp

http://www.damninteresting.com/?p=495

http://www.everything2.com/index.pl?node_id=643906

http://www.guardian.co.uk/food/story/0,,1576765,00.html

http://www.users.globalnet.co.uk/~aair/urticaria.htm

http://www.whyquit.com/whyquit/LinksJBlood.html

About the Illustrator

Roger Garcia

Roger Garcia immigrated to Canada from El Salvador at age of seven. Because of the language barrier, he had to find a way to communicate with other kids. That's when he discovered the art of tracing. It wasn't long before he mastered this highly skilled technique, and by age 14, he was drawing weekly cartoons for the "Edmonton Examiner."

He taught himself to paint and sculpt, and then in high school and college, Roger skipped class to hide in the art room all day in order to further explore his talent. Currently, Roger's work can be seen in a local weekly newspaper and in places around Edmonton, Alberta.

About the Author

Joanna Emery

Joanna Emery has always had a deep curiosity, a passion for history and a love of writing. She's enjoyed stories of the icky and fascinating things about the human body ever since her father, a forensic pathologist, used to tell her tales of body functions and dissected livers when she was a child. Joanna is the author of five children's books and numerous articles. She and her husband live with their three children, four cats, one guinea pig and five chickens, and they are currently building a small observatory in their backyard.

See Joanna's website at www.joannaemery.com.